INHERIT THE HUNT

A Journey into the Heart of American Hunting

Jim Posewitz

FALCON®

Guilford, Connecticut
An imprint of The Globe Pequot Press

Illustrations by Jim Stevens

Library of Congress Cataloging-in-Publication Data
Posewitz, Jim.
    Inherit the hunt : a journey into the heart of American hunting / Jim Posewitz.
        p.   cm.
    Includes bibliographical references.
    ISBN 1-56044-388-X (hardcover)
    1. Hunting~North America~History.   2. Wildlife conservation~North America~History.   I. Title.
SK40.P67   1999
799.2973~dc21   99-20454
                                                         CIP

Manufactured in the Unietd States of America
First edition/First paperback printing

This book is dedicated to a generation of people not yet born who will carry the desire to hunt in some mysterious configuration of their genetic make-up. Only they will know whether my generation kept the faith with our predecessors, and met the expectation of those who will be our heirs.

This writing is also dedicated to sons Brian, Allen, Carl, Matt, and Andrew—all enriched time spent hunting, fishing, camping, hiking, and sailing, the latter activity on some very marginal vessels. They carry the hunter's DNA and I believe that to be important.

Finally, this book is dedicated to a small bird that found its way to North America and stayed. A basic tenet of ethical hunting is to appreciate and utilize any animal killed. As a youth I killed an English sparrow. That act of killing has been on my mind for about a half century. By including the sparrow's role in telling this story, I hope to bring purpose to its sacrifice and a measure of peace to my heart.

ACKNOWLEDGMENTS

Thanks are due to Chris Cauble of Falcon Publishing for his editorial and organizational support as this project unfolded. Special thanks are also due to the editors of both words and ideas who helped this manuscript find its way: Ken Barrett, Dave Stalling, Ted Kerasote, Dan Crockett and Beth Kaeding. Thanks also to wildlife historian, author, and professor John Rieger for his review of an early draft of this work.

A special recognition is due my son Andrew who earned a degree in history and searched for many details necessary to this writing, but then I held his college loan. He was, however, cheerful throughout.

The family history was maintained by my brother John M. Posewitz and I thank him for that contribution. I also thank him and his wife Mary for hospitality and encouragement whenever it was needed. The character "Leroy" that appears in the text is Leroy Hiltgen now of Tilada, Wisconsin, who helped keep my youthful fantasy alive along the Pigeon River. I never have thanked him for skinning the skunk we caught our first winter as fox trappers.

Finally, special thanks to Gayle Joslin for support, encouragement, critical review and for keeping the wood stove going when I became preoccupied in the search for words to the neglect of basic chores.

While all these people provided valuable assistance the author retains full responsibility for both the concepts and details expressed in the telling of this story.

CONTENTS

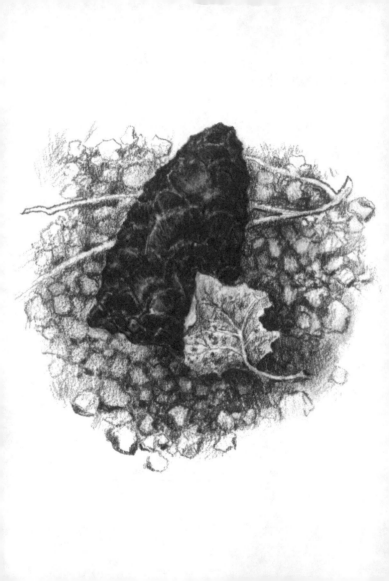

PREFACE

I was tired, hiking head down on a faint game trail toward a high saddle between two mountain peaks. As I plodded methodically upward, a shiny black object on the ground caught my eye. It was an object that forever changed my perception of my place as a North American hunter.

The six-mile hike, an annual event, was both a joy of summer and a check of my physical condition before the autumn hunting season. Now, a year past my sixtieth birthday and the cartilage pretty much worn out of one knee, I felt satisfied as I passed through stunted, wind-worn limber pine. My goal, the north face of 9,414-foot Crow Peak, was within view and within the energy left in me. This hike, in addition to improving my fitness, usually affords several hours of watching mountain goats once the high ridges are mounted.

The trek began in the ghost town of Elkhorn, a fading mining settlement that died when the ore played out. The dim trail toward the high country winds past abandoned miner cabins and mineral prospects, both fresh and old. Because broken glass and bits of metallic debris are common near the base of the mountain, I almost gave no thought to the slick edge of the object that caught the late morning sun and gave me a wink. But, honoring curiosity, I picked the shiny object from the pine duff and brushed it clean. And there it was, just lying in my hand, an obsidian arrow point, flaked on both sides. It is possible that the last human hands to hold it were those of a Stone Age wanderer some 9,000 years ago. It is certain that the hands that once held it—and the hands that held it now—belonged to a hunter.

I stared deep into the absolute blackness of the obsidian as I turned the ancient arrowhead in my hand. I wondered about the man who left it. A Stone Age traveler and now myself—hunters on the same ground. Thousands of years lay in the gulf between our times, but in a strange way the crafted stone I held and the instinct that brought me to the mountain connected us. A passion for the hunt has been a part of me since youth. Now, a half century after my first kill, an obsidian point confronts me with questions. How is it that I, a person of common means in a space age world, am a hunter? Where did this opportunity come from? Is there a responsibility that comes with it?

Hiking down the mountain, my mind traveled wildly and returned to trips taken into Central Asia and Western Europe. Those are places where few common people hunt, but places that hold reasons for telling this story. What I witnessed in these foreign lands were cultures where hunting by the common person has all but vanished.

Here in North America things are different. Here, at the close of the twentieth century, a very common hunter can still feel a physical and a spiritual linkage to a Stone Age hunter who left an arrow point on the shoulders of a Montana mountain. That ancient hunter and I had gone to the mountain for the same purpose.

The story of how all this came about lies strewn along a path as old as humanity. The trail of the hunt passed through some trying times on its way to our generation. There was a time when we almost lost it all in our pioneering exuberance. When the nineteenth century came to a close, a host of animals were perched on the edge of extinction. In the 100 years that followed, almost all the game species and many non-hunted species were restored to a wonderful abundance.

The richness of the restoration is universal. White-tailed deer again flash through the thickets of New Jersey's Pine Barrens while moose roam once more in the forests of Maine, New Hampshire, Vermont, and the Rocky Mountains from Wyoming to Alaska. The wild turkey calls from oak thickets and pine savannas all across the nation. Roosevelt elk drift like dark shadows through the heavy forests of Washington's Olympic Peninsula. Elk have returned to Pennsylvania, Kentucky, and Arkansas. Higher on the food chain, mountain lions are common throughout the West, and, on special nights, the wolf again sings to the northern moon. At the top of this pyramid of life, the grizzly bear is reclaiming a few of the habitats that haven't felt its presence for more than a century.

Having the abundance and diversity of wildlife we live with today is neither luck nor accident. It is the result of hard, purposeful work. It was work done by people of ordinary means and by people blessed with special talent and opportunity. What they had in common was that they chose to be hunters and there was room in our culture for anyone who made that choice. Today, those of us who hunt—and those who do not—need to appreciate and sustain this truth.

Some of the stories we need to tell go back to the earliest North American hunters. These ancient hunters survived because they were capable of killing hairy mammoths with no more than a wooden lance tipped with chipped stone. Scientists sorting the debris of ages in Europe, Asia, and Africa have found evidence of human tools and weapons going back 300,000 years. This telling of the story intercepts the trail of human hunters about 30,000 years ago and then skips through history, focusing on special events that influenced the unique nature of our hunting heritage.

The human transition from societies of hunters to civilized cultures with few hunters is a recent change in terms of human evolution. This change was rapid, and we hunters, for reasons we may not understand, are not ready to extinguish the wild ember of the hunt that burns within us. We find validity in the idea that our passion for the spirit of the chase needs to be sustained as part of our human diversity. We have been counseled that *the most important part of ecological tinkering is to save all the pieces.* Human hunters have been an indispensable piece of the ecosystems of earth since genesis. I believe we have a responsibility to preserve this particular element of human nature and nurture it, so it will remain functional in the process of evolution that still attends our kind.

Finally, this is a personal story about a kid of common means who wanted to hunt. My tale is not unique, far from it. It is the saga of hunters all across the continent. If you are a hunter, you may see yourself in these pages.

THE SPARROW

A half century has slipped away and it is hard to remember the detail. It was winter—winter in eastern Wisconsin, and chilled clouds of vapor were rolling in off Lake Michigan, layering ice onto every surface. Nothing escaped the damp and brutal artistry. Fishing and sailing boats were pulled out of the frozen harbor. Their rope and cable riggings caught the fog, stiffened, and locked rigid. Ice-laden power lines drooped ominously overhead. Each twig, each line in the rigging, each crackling wire—everything the damp fog touched thickened with ice.

The winter sun hung low in the December sky. Shining through the fog, the sun was ringed by a dim, rainbow-colored, crystal halo. Ice crystals suspended in the air sparkled and twinkled as an easy on-shore breeze pushed the frozen shroud inland. The world was simple—black, white, and the sun's faded halo.

The dampness was everywhere. It was a dampness that carried the cold through the wool outercoat, penetrated the flannel shirt, and finally sunk beneath the cotton long johns on its way to the marrow of one's bones. If you had to be still, you drew your muscles tight and took shallow breaths to try to keep the cold from the core of yourself. As the muscles wearied, the shivering started, usually in the knees, moving inward and upward to the shoulders, eventually reaching your spine. You feared that it, too, would rattle.

It was on such a day that I waited, motionless except for a knee quivering slightly out of control. I knew the birds would come, but I had to wait. The birds were always nearby, and they had been baited for days—their comings and goings noted with reasonable precision. The gun, Christmas-new, rested across my lap, and in carefully fashioned concealment, I waited for the birds

to come. Hours of practice had honed my skills as a shooter. Now I waited, cold—and confident.

Suddenly, they were there! Without warning the birds were in the air right in front of me, appearing out of nowhere, wings locked in swirling descent and then back to accelerated flight—in a flash, gone. I was not prepared for the swiftness of it all. Watching from a distance, there had seemed to be more time. Now, closer than I had ever been to them, it all seemed too fast and out of control. I was a stationary object, and they sailed past so close and sudden that there was no time to even shoulder the gun. Had they seen through my concealment?

In little more than a moment they were back, but this time they settled softly into the bait spread across the snow. While the birds pecked and gobbled the feed that lured them, I slowly brought up the gun, took careful aim at the nearest feeding bird . . . and fired!

In the cold, damp air, the gun's report was little more than a pop. Instantly the flock lifted, panicky thrashing wings filled the air, and, more suddenly than it began, I was once again—alone. No longer cold, but alone except for the feathered form fluttering weakly in the snow before me. In a moment, it lay still. I had executed my plan. I had, after considerable planning, preparation, and practice, gone out and purposefully killed an animal.

Quickly I rose from my stool, set aside my BB gun, swung the garage door open, and walked through the bread crumbs I had spread for bait. There, among the crumbs, lay a very dead English sparrow. A tiny speck of blood dotted the snow near its head. To this day I clearly remember picking up the bird, smoothing the feathers, and appreciating for the first time their composition and pattern. The little bird was warm in my palm, and I flexed a wing, marveling at how each feather assumed a position in the extended wing that made flight real.

The curiosity and wonder toward this little bird were genuine, but I didn't kill the sparrow because I was curious. I thought then and I think now, I killed because I wanted to be a hunter. Little did I realize that this singular event connected me to some Stone Age, fur-draped, Pleistocene hunter who had once, a very long time ago, rammed a spear into the heart of a mammoth.

❧❧❧

Being a hunter, or being a boy wanting to be a hunter, in eastern Wisconsin in the mid-1940s was not the easy choice. My father neither hunted nor fished. No relative in his generation hunted or fished. It was said that my grandfather, on my mother's side, once hunted on his brother's small dairy farm and that there was, somewhere in the family, a sixteen-gauge, double-barreled Stevens shotgun. These grand people were the immigrant generation of my family, and little was ever revealed about their history. Half the grandparents never learned to speak English, and my generation had little time for Lithuanian, the native tongue. Now, sadly, I realize that I never really knew them. I never even had a real conversation with half of them. The shotgun, however, was real, and in time, for a time, I claimed it. With it I killed a cottontail rabbit, a few grouse, a pheasant, and more than a few squirrels from wood lots around the county.

As for my parents' generation, they were athletes, and some, such as my father and his brother, were very good. They were Depression-era athletes who played part time and mostly for the love of the game and expenses. Our town had a professional basketball franchise and my father and uncle played for Ballhorn's of Sheboygan, Wisconsin. On February 13, 1935, one month before I was born, Ballhorn's beat the original

Celtics 34 to 33. My dad scored 22 points. The Celtics had come to town as the world champions. Ballhorn's was the local funeral parlor and still is.

Green Bay's Packer Stadium was an hour to the north, and the major league sports franchises of Milwaukee and Chicago were only a little farther to the south. Every Sunday of a Packer home game my father chartered a bus for local fans, and we watched Curly Lambeau coach, Don Hutson catch passes, Tony Canadeo run wide, and Ted Fritsch run up the middle. These sports heroes were the powerful influences in our culture—they were what fathers wished for their sons. Our mothers lit little candles in the church and prayed we wouldn't get hurt. I was a sickly infant and my mother once scrubbed that old church on her hands and knees so that I might get well. I did. Life was played out within a pretty tight triangle: my dad's gas station, Packer Stadium, and the Lithuanian church.

To aspire to be a hunter in that culture was not the path well traveled. My buddy Leroy and I ran a little trapline before dawn because the "after school" belonged to football, basketball, or baseball. Weekend hunting had to wait until after the games. In the 1940s there was little opportunity, and even less encouragement, to be a hunter or angler. Still, the desire was smoldering somewhere within my very being.

My father was a blue-collar businessman, and he provided well for us, running his own service station. It was the time before gasoline was self-service, and most customers asked for "a buck's worth" at nineteen and one-half cents a gallon. My father did not own the oil-patch, but his son could become a hunter and pursue an activity generally reserved for the world's royal and privileged classes. This was America, and the desire to be a hunter in this "New World" democracy was valid for anyone.

The life path along which the sparrow died soon began its rush through the years. Before long I would make my way to the fabulous hunting grounds of the Great Plains and Northern Rockies. It would be considerably later in life before I would wonder where the wildlife came from or how the privilege to pursue it found its way to me. When I sought those answers, I found and followed two trails back through time. One, the trail of the Stone Age hunter who brought the obsidian point to the Elkhorn Mountains. The other, the more familiar path of the later immigrants whose freedom produced the North American heroes who brought the hunting heritage to my generation.

The aboriginal hunters who crossed into North America over the Bering land bridge between 15,000 and 30,000 years ago left little sign. They were Stone Age hunters capable of killing the massive mammoths that crossed that plain with them. These first people of the continent lived as one with the animals that sustained them, and the land was richly endowed with fish and wildlife.

To this day, the descendants of the people who sent those hunters across the soggy tundra between Siberia and Alaska keep the story of that crossing alive within their culture. During the summer of 1994 on a trip into Kyrgyzstan in Central Asia, I was in an encampment of nomadic herdsmen. These distant cousins of the paleo-Indian hunters asked that I carry their greeting back to the native people of North America. I have.

The other branch of the trail of the North American hunter had to work its way through the dark castles of medieval Europe. Events that occurred beside the river Thames at Runnymede, England, were also destined to become part of the American hunter's history. It was there that white knights and black barons forged a charter with their king, a bargain won with the tips of their lances and the blades of their swords. The prize was the Magna Carta, a concession from the king that people other than kings could have rights.

Much later, the idea that all men should have the rights once reserved for royalty was brought across the Atlantic by leaders such as William Penn. These basic entitlements were among the rights that would be claimed and defended by common Americans from all walks of life. When one of those Americans stood up for his right to gather oysters on a New Jersey mud flat, we learned that the fish and wildlife of the new land belonged to all the people, as did the privilege to gather and eat these natural resources that we were now destined to hold in common.

The trail of our hunting heritage passed through Boston where tea went into the harbor and through a bitter winter at Valley Forge where 11,000 untrained men entered that encampment and, in the spring, 5,000 freedom fighters emerged to validate our Declaration of Independence.

Near the end of the nineteenth century, our hunter's trail passed through its own dark age, and the wildlife of an entire continent stared squarely into the eyes of oblivion. The renaissance began when a New Yorker went west to Medora, North Dakota, to ranch and to pursue what might have been the last big game animals of the United States. There can be no mistake about the blaze marks left on the hunter's trail when it passed through Medora, where a hunter who would be president drew perspective and inspiration. Theodore Roosevelt, a true conservation giant, stepped forward and said we could have wildlife in this country. Actually, he said without doubt, *we would have wildlife.* More importantly, he said that *wildlife would be for all of us.* He and his associates contemplated these things around hunters' campfires, and then they gave our conservation compass an absolutely superb heading.

In the wake of the Great Depression and the Dust Bowl years of the "dirty thirties," new leaders emerged. Visionary hunters, such as two from the conservation birthing grounds of the fertile Iowa plain—journalist Jay "Ding" Darling and scientist Aldo Leopold—stepped forward for wildlife and for all of us who would hunt. Darling was a tireless campaigner for wildlife restoration and first president on the National Wildlife Federation. He made things happen for wildlife on the political playing field. We remember Leopold as the father of game management, but he was more. Along the banks of the Wisconsin River, professor Leopold restored both a worn out piece of farmland and a run-down shack that has since become a type of shrine. There, Aldo Leopold's vision carried beyond the near horizon, and he told us how hunters could live in our nation's future with both grace and dignity. All these things and more happened, and, because they happened, the ember that burned inside of me stayed alive. Without the deeds of our hunter forefathers, the hunter's fire in me would have turned cold faster than a dead sparrow on a frozen lawn.

GOLDENEYE DUCKS
AND A RED-EYED FISH

As a boy of twelve, I crawled under a barbed-wire fence
into a cow pasture that bordered Wisconsin's Pigeon
River. My objective was to approach a flock of spring
migrant ducks that I had seen from a distance. Now I
stalked them—not to kill, but to see them better, to simply be closer.

The pasture was beaten, and "cow platters" were
something to avoid as I inched, belly to the ground,
toward the river. To the west, halfway across the state,
in a shack on the Wisconsin River, conservationist
Aldo Leopold may have been in the process of writing
A Sand County Almanac, or so I like to imagine. The
ducks flushed, pattering upstream, then took flight,
gained altitude, and circled back directly overhead. The
sky was blue and the ducks, common goldeneye, were a
crisp black and white, their wings whistling as they
passed overhead. When I rose to watch them go, a lone
drake mallard, his head a springtime-bright, iridescent
green, jumped from under an old willow that hung over
the river.

The memory of that moment and those birds

remains undiminished—its sights, sounds, and significance as sharp today as in the spring of 1947. I felt exceptionally privileged and realized that I was numbered among those who could not live without wild things. On that spot, I made a pledge to work for conservation and spend my life trying to preserve the wildness in our land and surely an ember of wildness burning within myself. At the time, I didn't know a thing about the learned Dr. Leopold, his shack on the Wisconsin River some 200 miles away, and the words he would leave that return time and time again to visit my mind:

> But to those whose hearts are stirred by the sound of whistling wings and quacking mallards, wildlife is . . . not merely an acquired taste; the instinct that finds delight in the sight and pursuit of game is bred into the very fiber of the race.[1]

As Wisconsin worked its way out of our nation's great economic depression, there was a lot of tired land and not much habitat for fish or wildlife in the 1940s. All I knew then was that I *had* to hunt, fish, and trap, and this tattered little river I stood beside was within the range of my bicycle.

One of the river's tiny tributaries was a pipe that bled a foul refuse into the river from an adjacent rendering plant. In time I learned that I could catch a rock bass on a yellow fly if I fished upstream from the pipe. It surprises me to remember that even though I never caught many fish, and a red-eyed rock bass was a prize, I put it back. I guess I did that because it was the only fish I knew would take a yellow streamer that resembled nothing, but that I had tied myself. I caught that fish often.

Below the pipe, the catch was bullheads. In the spring we fished for suckers coming out of Lake Michigan. During the summer, my brother, his friends, and I would move rocks around in the riverbed, making wing dams and other structures that we hoped rock bass and other fish would accept. We always worked upstream from the foul pipe. In the fall, my buddy Leroy and I would trap muskrats and pretend we were in some wild place in Canada, Alaska, or the Northern Rockies catching marten, lynx, and wolverine. Our fish and wildlife world was pretty much limited to muskrats, suckers, bullheads, and the rock bass that would attack a simple yellow streamer. At that time our county had no deer, and we hunted hard to take a rabbit, squirrel, or pheasant. I sought an education from the outdoor magazines, and from the depth of that remembrance I recall an article about deer hunting prospects stating, "there are no deer in Kansas."

Our outdoor activities were tolerated as "surely better than the trouble some kids get into these days." The quote is from my mother, who baked wonderful bread and rolls, the source of the crumbs used to bait the sparrow. The smell of Saturday morning, the baking day, lingers. The comfort and warmth created in those post-Depression years was like an infant's first blanket. The security of it all, however, was no match for the whisper within myself that said . . . *go.*

At eighteen I left Wisconsin, pursuing the dreams of youth, an education, and a life in association with wild things and wild places. While I fled to Montana in 1953, my brother stayed to raise his edition of the next generation in central Wisconsin, and the change that soon swept over the old home ground became another classic piece of what was happening continent wide.

Where my generation fished for suckers and bull-head, my brother's children pursued coho and chinook salmon. The spring runs of suckers received little attention because steelhead trout surged up those same streams. My immigrant granduncle's tired dairy farm became part of Wisconsin's Kettle Moraine State Forest. The rocky pasture, a hog pen, and corn patch that are lodged in my memory quickly became a grassland with an encroaching hardwood forest. It is a forest edge now rich in grouse and white-tailed deer. My brother's sons routinely brought fat young bucks to the family meat hooks from the oak ridges and fir thickets of the Kettle Moraine. Young bucks and young hunters, savoring a richness of place and spirit, unaware of the tired poverty that had visited those same hills and streams in the days of their father and grandfathers.

I remember the poverty of the place during my generation's youth. The hog pen was nothing but a wooden fence surrounding a few mud-mired boulders; the corn patch defined by hand-piled, stone fence lines; and beyond, a rock-strewn pasture. My granduncle died before I knew him, so we knew the place as Aunt Eva's farm. I remember it as a happy, callous-generating piece of the earth. Now, all these years later, it occurs to me that the joy this immigrant generation felt came from hope and the freedom to be toiling for themselves.

My relatives were farming the rubble shoved south by the leading edge of the Wisconsin Glacier. I never heard how they came to pick that place, but a lifetime of labor was invested there. As dairy farmers they never had much of a chance. This, however, was the immigrant generation, and their crop included the new freedom that made the whole venture priceless. Still, it was a good day when the state of Wisconsin came with a deal for the farm. The land healed quickly, the people rested, and white-tailed deer took to the restored wildness of the Kettle Moraine State Forest.

The massive glacier that had shoved the rubble that became Aunt Eva's farm had bound up so much water as ice that it lowered the northern seas and exposed the Bering Plain between Siberia and Alaska. The plain was a land bridge between the continents, and it opened North America to wildlife from Eurasia. Of course, the wildlife did not come alone. Aboriginal hunters of the late Pleistocene followed the reindeer, bison, and mammoths onto this continent.

THE RISE AND FALL OF THE BERING BRIDGE

Archeology is the study of ancient people and cultures by finding and analyzing artifacts, paintings, monuments, and other remains. From the findings of archeologists we gain an understanding of our present circumstance by learning where we came from and how we learned to live within the natural rhythms of our own evolution. At times, these scientific hunters follow a hot trail, such as pursuing the lifestyle of an ancient pharaoh. Pharaohs had a lot of stuff, and when they died they tried to take it with them. A colder, more subtle trail is tracing the movements of the prehistoric hunters of the northern tundra. These ancestors of ours marked their passing with little more than a few stone tools and the ashes of campfires that went out 10,000 years ago.

The scientific detectives on the trail of North America's earliest hunters follow a cold trail, and what they discover is open to analysis and debate. There is no debate that what they have found is fascinating.

Somewhere in a distant past, during a period of cold climate called the Late Pleistocene, continental glaciers swelled to monstrous proportions, storing enormous volumes of water as solid ice. As a result, ocean levels gradually fell more than 100 feet, and, in the northern Pacific, a large, sweeping, shallow plain was exposed. The plain reached eastward from Siberia and westward from the Bering region of Alaska, and for thousands of years it linked the continents. Animals and hunters from Eurasia occupied this expansive plain of grass and muskeg, now named Beringia or the Bering Bridge.

Archeologists believe the native people of interior North America developed from the distant stock of Asiatic Mongol hunters who trekked across Beringia.

The hunters coming to this continent brought stone-tipped spears, tools chipped from stone, and implements fashioned from the bones of animals. They were hunters pursuing reindeer, mammoth, horses, steppe antelope, and other sub-arctic animals on the tundra and plain of Beringia. They were probably quite unaware that they were migrating to a new continent where they would find camels, sloths, saber-toothed cats, huge longhorn bison, and a short-faced bear that would dwarf any bear that now walks on earth.[2] This theory of ancestry and migration is supported by fragments of physical evidence and in the stories remembered and passed through generations of Central Asian people.

The Bering Bridge remained open until the enormous glaciers came to a stop and began to melt. The icy monolith that was the Wisconsin Glacier pushed heaps of rock and rubble before it as it shoved its way south from the Arctic. When it stopped, the debris came to rest on the very spot where my granduncle Peter and grandaunt Eva Yekenevicz would, 10,000 years later, invest a lifetime of toil. Until now we never recognized it as the place where an icy hand of creation ran out of energy and began to recede. To us, the place was simply Aunt Eva's farm.

Slowly the glaciers' melting waters restored the depleted seas. In the eye of the imagination, there must have been a day on the plain of Beringia when an ebbing tide no longer ebbed enough, a day when a hunter or family of hunters were no longer able to return to a traditional campsite, their passage barred by a channel full of rolling blocks of ice and swirling slush. My mind's eye sees two hunters looking at one another across the surging tidal rush, perhaps signaling in some primitive way that they would return on the next ebb tide and try again to unite. Both hunters turn and walk away, one to his camp to the east, the other to a similar camp to the west, each carrying a spear tipped with a stone point made by flaking both sides of a hard stone.

At least ten thousand years would pass before the two camps would meet again. A hundred centuries or more would pass before humans from the Old World would again bridge the sea, this time bringing their genius for progress to North America. The Europeans would come with metal, muskets, wheels, and a new God. The aboriginal hunters of North America would carry bows and stone-tipped arrows, use a travois to move their gear, revere the earth as mother, and dance to the power of the sun.

⋘⋙⋘⋙

Isolated from Europe and Asia, the Pleistocene inhabitants of North America pursued their own evolutionary direction and pace. The humans of the Old World did likewise. The difference in direction and pace created the European history with which most of us are familiar. It is a history reconstructed from rich archeological evidence, preserved through the genius of alphabets, recorded in scripture, and stored in universities far older than the nations of North America. Most, if not all, of these advances were born of a leisure from hunting and gathering, using time made available through the domestication of plants and animals.

Long before technology enabled them to again travel between the continents, the people of the Old World went through a significant change in how they lived with the earth. The change, though gradual, was dramatic. In its simplest explanation it involved taking control over the food supplies that dictated human survival. The development of agriculture made food supplies more predictable and more reliable. As that occurred the people had time to pursue other curiosities, and the creative genius of humans was released. This genius found expression in invention, discovery, culture, commerce, and warfare. Wildlife and hunting persisted, but hunting was generally not maintained as an activity of the common people. Rather, hunting usually became a sport reserved for royalty and for the training of warriors. Under various forms of royal protection, many sporting species survived through the centuries, but the terms of that survival were harsh.

WHITE KNIGHTS,
BLACK BARONS, AND KINGS

Space age technology allows us to view the earth as a blue planet alive in the cosmic chaos of barren landscapes, hostile rocks, swirling gasses, and the frozen dirt balls of streaking comets. This unique planet must have worn a visible frozen lid when the massive glaciers covered extensive portions of earth.

The melting glaciers and rising seas that reflooded the land bridge between Alaska and Siberia also must have raised water levels in the English Channel. The British Isles thus became more isolated from the European continent. It is estimated that between 300 and 400 Stone Age hunters made up the human population of those islands in the late Pleistocene. During the period that followed, the human population of the islands grew to about three or four thousand. For these people the main subsistence animal was the red deer, which may have been domesticated as part of the survival strategy. By 1700 B.C., the production of grains, the clearing of forests, and a growing dependence on domestic sheep characterized the evolving and growing human society.

We look to the British Isles because English common law eventually influences the development of our legal footing as North American citizen hunters. The portion of the hunter's trail that traveled this route from the seventh through the nineteenth centuries covered rocky ground for those who would be hunters. We need to visit that period and that perilous trail to find the wisdom visible in the ashes of time. It is a wisdom that could enable us to avoid the consequences that fell upon both the hunters and the hunted of those once wild isles.

Most legal scholars in England and elsewhere build the basic foundation of wildlife law on principles found in early Roman law. The basic Roman idea was that wild animals by their very nature do not have an owner. Another basic concept was that wildlife could belong to the person who could take (kill) or control (capture) them. Thus, through the process of taking, wildlife could become the possession of an individual as a matter of personal right. Personal rights, however, always have been dependent upon whatever form of government people either endure or enjoy.

As England approached modern times, the government was a succession of kings. The king's interest in wildlife, land, and individual rights was intense and usually selfish. As a rule, kings kept the good stuff for themselves. Some of the early laws relating to game were laid down by Ine, King of Wessex, who enacted forest laws as early as the year 693. In 1016 the game law of King Canute prevented the common people or peasants from hunting on the king's land. The penalty for violation was simple enough: death.

The idea of killing an individual to protect a privileged person's claim to wild animals as private property had a way of persisting, even into relatively modern times. Prior to the Norman Conquest, Britain oriented toward Scandinavia with regard to its laws and outlook. Following the Norman Conquest in 1066 however, the orientation was toward central Europe with regard to game laws and hunting. The Norman touch was simple: all property in wildlife was reserved for the king. The king designated others who could avail themselves of the privilege. Those others were the nobility and the clergy. But, it was the king, as the sovereign, who maintained control over the wild animals, and it was the king who gave others permission to hunt them.

Through the centuries some kings addressed the taking of their game animals rather harshly. William I enforced the forest laws with punishments that ranged from mutilation to death. One historian noted the following as an example of a penalty: "Whoever shall kill a stag, a wild boar, or even a hare shall have his eyes torn out."[3] In the time of kings Richard I and John, forest laws were administered by a civil service, an early version of a bureaucracy of the hunt.

The revolt of English barons in 1215 led to the signing of the Magna Carta, a document that confirmed the feudal rights of the barons. Thus it was that a few dozen barons gathered on the green at Runnymede on the banks of the Thames, and there secured for themselves the concession that they possessed rights by virtue of their existence. More importantly, these rights were independent of the king's will. Five centuries later, American revolutionaries would cite the Magna Carta as the source of their own *natural rights* necessary for the building of new nations.[4]

King John died during this war. His successor Henry III was forced to address a festering dissatisfaction against the forest laws. The result was a Forest Charter, a kind of amendment to the Magna Carta, issued in 1216, which contained the following:

No man shall from henceforth lose either life or member for killing of our deer; but if any man be taken and convicted for taking of our venison, he shall make a grievous fine, if he hath anything whereof.[5]

Noteworthy is the use of the possessive terminology, *our deer* and *our venison.* There was no doubt that while the moderately benevolent barons saw the injustice in the degree of punishment, they also clearly retained wildlife as their property. The notion of the commoner as hunter was quite remote. It is also apparent that the commoner was not really expected to ever have much in the way of assets.

The royalty retained a robust fondness for wildlife. It was recorded that Henry III hosted a Christmas dinner that included 430 red deer, 200 fallow deer, 200 roe deer 200 wild swine, 1,300 hare, 450 rabbits, 2,100 partridges, 290 pheasants, and 395 swans. The peasants, likewise, retained a fondness for wildlife, and poaching continued for both food and markets. In 1293 the English Parliament, in an attempt to stem poaching, decreed:

No actions were to be taken against officials (foresters, parkers, warreners) who kill poachers who resisted arrest.[6]

In 1389 during the reign of Richard II, it was decreed that the pursuit of game was restricted to those qualified by the ownership of land. The decree denied any person without a proper landholding the right to even possess dogs or equipment used in taking game.

This class warfare went on for centuries, often with considerable intensity. By the early 1600s, while some Europeans were carving footholds in North America, back in England they continued to fight one another for access to wildlife. England had a civil war of its own in the middle of that century, and, without the protection of the monarchy, some of the forest laws were repealed. The taking of game was rampant, and walls around royal hunting grounds were breached. The English restored their monarchy in 1671 out of either a fondness for royalty or for the security of order. Charles II quickly instituted a gentleman's game privilege based on land ownership. Thus, the struggle for equal access to wildlife continued unabated. Poaching and game markets remained socially acceptable among the disenfranchised, while the aristocracy continued to war against the people taking game.

Gamekeepers in the employ of the privileged were empowered to seize dogs, guns, and hunting equipment and to search suspect's homes. If an offender happened to be killed in the process of protecting the royal's game, the gamekeeper was immune from prosecution. About the time the North American colonists were contemplating an uprising of their own, an organized poaching operation known as the Waltham Gang, operating with blackened and masked faces, was taking game from Farnham and Waltham Chase. Those who were caught and convicted were jailed, fined, and pilloried. The conflict intensified into class warfare that included murder and, at least in the view of royalty, one particularly heinous crime—the theft of a shipment of French wine intended for the Prince of Wales. The aristocracy countered with passage of the Black Act that restored capital punishment for poaching. At the time of the American Revolution, legally authorized hunters in England constituted less that one-half of one percent of the population, and poaching was the major rural crime.

In England, the conflict between the landed gentry and the citizens who would take wild game for subsistence, sale, or sport persisted long after the colonization of North America. It is probable that while American folk hero Daniel Boone was relishing his natural freedom to stalk deer in the forests of Kentucky and Tennessee, his brethren of the hunt were being flogged for doing the same in the forests of England. While Boone was hunting and the Brits were flogging, the people of Boston threw English tea into the harbor.

In England, conflict, poaching, capital punishment, and whippings continued through the next two centuries—just as they had for the previous eleven. Royal gamekeepers eagerly adopted new enforcement technology, including spring guns and mantraps capable of incapacitating or killing poachers.

In Britain, the idea of the common hunter as part of a populist conservation movement never germinated. While the class feud between people of privilege and people of common means went on, six species of large mammals on the British Isles slipped into the black nothingness of extinction: the wolf, brown bear, beaver, wild boar, reindeer, and aurochs.

As the twentieth century approached its end, the class struggle continued as Britain's Parliament debated the prohibition of fox hunting. In England, a foxhunt included the hunter, the hounds, the fox, and the League Against Cruel Sports. These contemporary hunters were once described by Oscar Wilde as "the unspeakable in full pursuit of the uneatable." In reporting on the perennial debate to ban the hunt, the Associated Press noted:

Hunt enthusiasts say at least some of the anti-fox-hunting lobby's fury springs from resentment of the sport's image as a pursuit of the landed gentry.[7]

In November 1997, Britain's House of Commons voted to ban the hunting of foxes and other wildlife by an overwhelming margin, 411 to 151. A parliamentary scheduling problem prevented the legislation's immediate implementation. In December of that year the Associated Press reported that masked protesters attacked a crowd gathered for a fox hunt. The protesters were using "clubs, staves and iron bars and they attacked anybody who offered any resistance." Thirty-one people were arrested and six were injured. All the injured were hunters.

FOUR HUNDRED YEARS
OF CHAOS

On October 12, 1492, Christopher Columbus stepped upon the beach of Watling Island in the Bahamas. When he did, the Europeans were forced to accept the idea that the world was round. The impact of his discovery was considerably greater on the aboriginal hunters of North America.

For the North American Indians, the *Pinta, Nina,* and *Santa Maria* carried the horsemen of the apocalypse. The Native Americans had been isolated from Europe and Asia since the withering ice age replenished the seas. For 10,000 years, the Native American people either remained substantially hunters or fashioned agricultural economies augmented by hunting and gathering. Suddenly, one hundred centuries later, they were in the company of strange people carrying the leading edge of human technology.

For the Europeans, it was an irresistible opportunity to build an empire, and the builders came with metal, gunpowder, and a God commanding them to colonize. In 1496, King Henry VII commissioned John Cabot to discover a new trade route to Asia, and the next year

Cabot and his son Sebastian reached the east coast of North America.[8] Their eyes looked excitedly upon a new world. Staring back at them from the forest edge were hunters, who must have thought them alien beings.

The immigrants coming ashore carried technology developed by people who had become proficient at domesticating crops and animals, living in complex sedentary communities, making metal, trading on an intercontinental scale, and waging war. The new arrivals came to colonize a land occupied by tribes of people living mostly as hunter-gatherers in reasonable harmony with nature. The ecological changes that occurred as a result of this new settlement quickly eclipsed the impact brought to this continent by the ancient migrations of animals and hunters across the plain of Beringia so long ago.

This time the bridge facilitating the new migration was the sturdy little vessels that delivered immigrants. Their ships of wood, iron, canvas, and hemp carried the technological progress of centuries as well as the burning embers of unfulfilled human aspirations. Within their hearts, the immigrants carried the quest for freedom, notions of natural rights, and, in some, the seed of rebellion. Those coming from the British Isles also brought early Roman notions of what was wild and some important legal remnants of the deal struck at Runnymede. Most likely a few of the new arrivals carried residual scars from the royal lash, possibly applied for humbly snaring rabbits on the hunting grounds of kings.

As European settlers gained tenuous footholds in North America, they found a forested shoreline rich in game, estuaries alive with waterfowl, and river deltas teeming with fish. To the colonists, hunting, fishing, and gathering natural foods quickly became routine. The degree to which it was held a right and the degree to which it was a necessity mattered little. It is significant, however, that back in England, seventeenth century philosophers were defining the terms of the social evolution that was occurring. One such person, John Locke, advanced an idea that was particularly suited to the pioneering culture in the colonies. Locke's ethical standard, viewed as a source of the American natural rights tradition, simply was: "all people were equal and free before God and each other."[9]

Locke's thinking was a strong influence in the developing colonies. The Declaration of Independence of

1776 was described as "the fullest flowering . . . of the natural rights philosophy."[10] This "flowering" marked the end of the trail for centuries of royal power and privilege.

The importance of wildlife was frequently affirmed in the evolving American culture. When William Penn arrived in Pennsylvania in 1682 he noted:

The food, the woods yield, is your elks, deer, raccoons, beaver, rabbits, turkeys, pheasants, heathbirds, pidgeons, and partredge innumerably; we need no setting dogs to ketch, they run by droves into the house in cold weather.[11]

In later correspondence Penn added:

Our rivers have also plenty of excellent fish and water foul as sturgeon, roe shad, herring, cadfish, or flatheads, sheeps heads, roach and perch; and trout in inland streams. Of foule, the swan, white, gray and black goose and brads, the best duck and teal I ever eate and the snipe and curloe with the snow bird are also excellent.[12]

The related idea that wildlife was for all the people did not escape William Penn. In his Charter for the Commonwealth of 1683, he included the "liberty to fowl and hunt upon the lands they hold, and all other levels therein not enclosed (and) to fish in all waters in the said land."[13]

Penn's language carried a clear expression of both the necessities and beliefs about New World freedoms. However, it would eventually fall upon the people of New Jersey to find the direction for the nation. It was out on the New Jersey meadowlands, at the mouth of the Raritan River, where the critical questions of wildlife ownership and the public trust responsibility of the states were decided.

The whole business began on the 12th day of March

1664 when King Charles II of England made a land grant to his brother James, the Duke of York. James was given a big piece of the New World that included the Raritan River. It wasn't exactly a grant since the duke and his heirs were required:

> to yield and render . . . yearly and every year, forty beaver-skins, when they shall be demanded, or within ninety days after.[14]

King Charles II was indeed a generous man, for in addition to the land, he gave his brother the following:

> We do further . . . grant unto our said dearest brother, James . . . full and absolute power . . . to correct, punish, pardon, govern and rule all . . . subjects of us . . . as shall . . . adventure themselves into . . . or . . . inhabit within the same.[15]

The Minute Men and other freedom-loving colonists would eventually change these conditions, but some of the other details in the land grant stayed with the real estate and would haunt the judicial system of the new nation for some time. Of direct concern to hunters, anglers, and oyster gatherers of the new nation would be specifics of the king's generous gift that included exclusive rights to "marshes, waters, lakes, fishings, hawkings, huntings and fowlings."[16]

Through the next century and a half there were social upheavals as well as orderly changes that included land sales involving many individual owners. Disputes over the validity of the king's grant to the duke were inevitable. The New Jersey dispute was about oysters near the mouth of the Raritan on meadowlands consisting of saltwater swamps and marshes. Arguments frequented those lands as adjacent landowners filled in the swamps, built wharves over the marshes, and otherwise developed docks and harbors. The importance of the lawsuits about these lands was noted as early as 1821 when a New Jersey Supreme Court justice observed:

> It is a fact, as singular as it was unexpected, that the taking of a few bushels of oysters . . . should involve . . . questions momentous in their nature as well as in their magnitude . . . affecting the rights of all our citizens, and embracing in their investigations, the laws of nations; and of

England, the relative rights of Sovereign and subjects, as well as the municipal regulations of our own country.[17]

Twenty-one years later the U.S. Supreme Court resolved the questions of who owned the oysters, the meadowlands, and, in essence, the fish and wildlife of America. The particular question involved whether or not a riparian landowner could exclude others from taking oysters from the estuary of the Raritan River. The case, brought by a Mr. Merritt Martin, was also a test of how English wildlife law might apply in the United States. In 1842 the Supreme Court ruled:

When the people of New Jersey took possession of the reins of government, and took into their own hands the powers of sovereignty, the prerogatives and regalities which before belonged either to the crown or the parliament, became immediately and rightfully vested in the state.[18]

This judicial foundation—and other court rulings that followed—supports state (public) ownership of wildlife, subject to rights surrendered to the general (federal) government. The king's power of sovereignty fortunately had been tempered by the Magna Carta. The monarchy retained power over wild animals; however, it was a privilege with a responsibility. The responsibility was to hold those assets in trust for the people. In North America, the important transfer of that responsibility came when the court passed the trustee's role to the states. The concept of "public trust" is based on the principle that there are some things so valuable to all of us that they cannot be owned by any individual. In the United States, air, water, fish, and wildlife are such common possessions.

The idea of common ownership of wild resources and trustee management of those resources came with hard lessons. As our pioneering culture spread westward, wildlife experienced its own equivalent of the Dark Ages. It was a darkness from which species like the passenger pigeon and Audubon's sheep would not emerge. Subsistence hunting and commercial killing of any wild animal that could be eaten or marketed was a plague upon our new land. The dramatic and unforgettable symbol of this tragedy was the buffalo.

The beginning of the nineteenth century was marked with a notation that Colonel John Kelly had killed the last bison in Pennsylvania. The year was 1801.[19] The buffalo that Kelly killed was of the species of bison that came to North America across the Bering plain in the company of the Pleistocene hunters. The buffalo and their accompanying human and animal predators had sustained a reasonable relationship for at least fifteen centuries.

Buffalo ranged from the Canadian sub-arctic to Mexico. They lived in inter-mountain valleys along the Rockies and extended their range eastward to the Atlantic. At one time there may have been one hundred million of these durable and adaptable animals. The analysis of their demise will continue, and perhaps in time we will understand it all. There is little doubt, however, that one of the more dramatic chapters of the sad saga of buffalo and of the people of the buffalo was played out in Montana. It occurred as the nineteenth century was rushing toward dramatic conclusion.

In the mid-1800s, the railroads that had already hauled buffalo hides and parts out of the southern plains had not yet penetrated the western edge of the northern Great Plains. Here the practical method of transport was the Missouri River, and the hide and tongue killers packed their booty to Fort Benton,

Montana Territory, the upper limit of steamboat navigation. The river town was pressing pioneers and progress into the last sanctuary of remoteness in what would be the lower forty-eight states. The steamboat's down-river leg carried the spoils of our commercial war on wildlife to the wharves of St. Louis. Bales of buffalo hides and the stench of death dominated the riverfront.

It was on the sprawling grasslands west of the great American heartland where the tragic lesson of unrestrained exploitation of wildlife became most brutally visible and grimly documented. The last act of this continent-wide drama was played out on the land of the Sioux, the Crow, and the Blackfeet, where grasslands turned blood red, buffalo skulls bleached white, and pilgrim "bone pickers" gathered the remaining evidence for fertilizer. *We had taken our wildlife and turned it over to commerce for decisions about its future.* In the end, it was the bone pickers who symbolized the bottom line, and the bottom line was $7 per ton paid for buffalo bones delivered to Miles City, Montana Territory, in 1884.[20] The northern plains fell deathly silent, and from the depth of that silence emerged the first voices calling for wildlife's renaissance. When the voices came, they were voices from hunters.

Montana became a territory in 1864, and from the beginning, laws to protect fish and wildlife were passed by pioneer legislators. The people saw the crimes, and those in responsible positions tried to stop the commercial killing. The first comprehensive game law in Montana Territory passed in 1871. It closed the season on bison in specified areas, and in 1876 a law was passed making it illegal to kill a bison for its hide and waste the meat.[21] In 1874 the U.S. Congress had also passed a bill to prevent the useless slaughter of buffalo, but President Ulysses S. Grant, on the military advice of General Sherman, vetoed the measure. The Montana law and similar laws of other western territorial legislatures of that period were progressive, and they demonstrated a conservation ethic among the pioneers. The territories, however, lacked any enforcement structure, and the laws were ineffective.

With the demise of the buffalo, the market hunters turned their attention to other game animals to feed miners rushing to western gold fields. The wildlife resources continued its drift toward extinction. In Montana, the leading legislative advocates for stopping the killing and bringing a sense of stewardship to wildlife management were the brothers, James and

Granville Stuart. These men were ranchers and miners, and Granville's biography noted that he was also an avid waterfowl hunter.

In 1876 the United States celebrated its first centennial. In the West, the celebration was tempered by events both dramatic and brutal. Out on the northern plains, the hot summer of that year was destined to become a landmark year in the history of the Montana Territory. While futile legislative attempts to temper the buffalo slaughter were being enacted in Bannock, the territorial capital, the total number of buffalo hides shipped down the Missouri from Fort Benton peaked at 80,000. In June, along the Little Bighorn River, the most memorable battle in the struggle for the American West occurred. Sitting Bull, Crazy Horse, and the warriors who followed their leadership engaged and annihilated George Armstrong Custer and the troopers of the 7th Cavalry. However, neither this act of desperation by the aboriginal buffalo hunters of the plains nor the legislative protestation of the pioneering residents could stem the commerce in buffalo. The killing of buffalo stopped only when there were no more buffalo to be killed. By 1884, the buffalo shipments from Fort Benton had dropped to zero, and a deathly silence settled over the high plains.[22]

The Native Americans who had come across the Bering plain with the buffalo thousands of years ago were now alone, and the land that was their mother was strange to them. In this time of despair, the Oglalas sent three men—Good Thunder, Brave Bear and Yellow Breast—west to see a Paiute holy man. The holy man told them how to bring back the buffalo, save the Indian people, and make the *Wasichus* (white man) disappear. The Oglalas were told a new world was coming, and:

> It would come in a whirlwind out of the west and would crush out everything on this world, which was old and dying. In that other world there was plenty of meat, just like old times; and in that world all the dead Indians were alive, and all the bison that had ever been killed were roaming around again.[23]

The Holy Man gave the emissaries of the Sioux a sacred red paint, two eagle feathers, and a dance. The dance was the Ghost Dance. The new dance was a petition in a time of desperation for people keeping hope alive when so much of what they cherished was dying. They had been hunters for as long as they had been people, and the rhythms of life as they knew it were collapsing. If they could only be heard, they would be delivered from the blue-coated soldiers, the miners swarming their sacred hills, the settlers taking the land, and the new "white father" whose words could not be trusted. If they could be heard, they would be delivered to the new world where the *Wasichus* would not be allowed to go, and so they danced the new dance.

❦❦❦

Colonel Kelly shot the last buffalo in Pennsylvania when the nineteenth century was one year old. As this turbulent century approached its end, the American Indians killed a colonel named Custer in a desperate effort to save the lifestyle of people who were one with the buffalo on the western plains. As the twentieth century approached, another Pennsylvanian, Pittsburgh hunter John Phillips, tracked a white-tailed buck through the snow for three days before killing the deer. During that odyssey he saw no other deer tracks and told a friend, "I am done, I think I have killed the last deer in Pennsylvania."[24]

Continent wide, it was wildlife's darkest hour.

THEODORE ROOSEVELT
AND THE COMMON HUNTER

While the tragic events involving people, wildlife, and the land ran their course throughout the American West, a remarkable New Yorker took up residence in North Dakota. He was a man in search of adventure. He had a taste of the vanishing frontier and experience as a western stockman. We remember and celebrate him as the man who defined the terms for wildlife recovery in North America.

Theodore Roosevelt was a hunter, and he exercised that passion during the decade that saw buffalo shipments down the Missouri River drop to zero, the Sioux dance the Ghost Dance, and the brutal blizzards of 1886-87 destroy the myths of open-range cattle grazing on the high plains of North America. Roosevelt spent a great deal of time in pursuit of what must certainly have appeared to be the last of North America's big game. Traveling from his North Dakota ranch by saddle horse, pack string, and wagon, he probed the deep corners of extensive wild lands for the vanishing virgin abundance of big game. In 1884, Roosevelt went deep into Wyoming's Bighorn Mountains in pursuit of his first elk and found them two days travel beyond the ranches of advancing civilization. In those same mountains he killed a grizzly bear. In 1886, he hunted bighorns in wild rugged lands near his ranch and penetrated the Bitterroot Mountains on the Idaho-Montana border to hunt moose. That same year he embarked on a particularly arduous mountain goat hunt in northern Idaho. In 1887, he successfully hunted caribou deep in the Selkirk Mountains of British Columbia.

In 1889, the very same year the Sioux were given the Ghost Dance, Roosevelt spent days searching for a herd

of wild buffalo rumored to be near the headwaters of Montana's Wisdom River. He found them in Idaho just beyond the Montana border, and he killed a large bull. He wrote of that moment:

I gazed on these bison, themselves part of the last remnant of a doomed and nearly vanished race. Few, indeed, are the men who now have, or ever more shall have, the chance of seeing the mightiest of American beasts, in all his wild vigor, surrounded by the tremendous desolation of his far-off mountain home.[25]

Roosevelt, it seems, knew he was in pursuit of something that may have been doomed. However, a conservation ethic also was emerging in Roosevelt as he pursued his adventures on the outer edges of advancing civilization. The following account of the relationship between the hunter and his guide, John Willis, is an example:

On this trip Theodore talked constantly to Willis, who made his living by slaughtering game for their hides, about the necessity for conserving wildlife. Although he would not admit it at the time, Theodore had made of him a staunch believer in conservation and he thereafter not only ceased to be a game butcher but became a strong worker for its preservation.[26]

I imagine that Theodore Roosevelt spent long hours staring into the embers of his hunter's fire. It is probable that during these same hours, the Sioux gathered to dance the Ghost Dance deep into the same black nights. The Native American hunters and a *Wasichu* hunter beneath the same celestial dome. The blackness of space decorated by a stellar magnificence embracing them all. And, in the season of hunting, a sky dominated by a constellation the Greeks knew as Orion, the Hunter. It is possible to imagine those nights as a time when the fate of North America's wildlife was passing through a veil, passing from the custody of descendants of Pleistocene mammoth hunters to the progeny of those who had just freed themselves from the tyranny of kings. From Roosevelt's contemplative hours, a wildlife conservation ethic emerged to form the pillars of the North American hunting ethic. The bedrock components of that ethic were preserving and restoring the game and doing it for all the people—equally.

While it is a simple formula, it is impossible to exaggerate the importance of its parts. Within this simple ethic is the fiber of democracy that enabled me, a blue-collar boy born a half century later in the midst of the great economic depression, to grow into a hunter. Within this formula is the trust our democracy places in *we the people.* Within this formula is the faith that common people can work in common cause. Finally, within this formula was the hope that we would do what must be done to bring the wildlife back to abundance—for all the people.

Writing before the end of the nineteenth century, Theodore Roosevelt saw North American hunting as something out of the dim and distant European past, in his words, "before history dawned." Of more relevance, however, was his firm belief that on this side of the Atlantic, hunting opportunity and the conservation responsibility that came with it could be for everyone. In an article published in 1893, Roosevelt wrote:

> . . . hunters, who . . . penetrated . . . this wilderness, found themselves in . . . hunting grounds . . . much the same as their lusty barbarian ancestors followed, with weapons of bronze and of

iron, in the dim years before history dawned. As late as the end of the seventeenth century, the turbulent village nobles of Lithuania and Livonia hunted the bear, the bison, the elk, the wolf, and the stag, and hung the spoils in their smoky wooden palaces: and so, *two hundred years later, the free hunters of Montana . . . hunted game almost or quite the same in kind, through the cold mountain forests . . .* (emphasis added)[27]

Of particular importance is Roosevelt's recognition that the activity of nobles in the Old World could now be available to the . . . *free hunters.* The necessity for a democratic approach to both the conservation of wildlife and access to wildlife was a recurring theme with Roosevelt. In 1905 he addressed the process of keeping North American forests and wildlife from destruction by stating:

. . . above all else, we should realize that the effort toward this end is essentially a democratic movement. It is . . . in our power . . . to preserve large tracts of wilderness . . . and to preserve game . . . for . . . all lovers of nature, and to give reasonable opportunities for the exercise of the skill of the hunter, whether he is or is not a man of means.[28]

On another occasion he stated it as follows:

The movement for the conservation of wild life, and the larger movement for the conservation of all our natural resources, are essentially democratic in spirit, purpose and method.[29]

Theodore Roosevelt was a man of means, and he could have easily busied himself pursuing the last remnants of prized wild animals as the frontier was civilized. He also could have focused on protecting game for his own use behind his own fences. His greatness, however, was in the fact that he saw himself as a member of a community of hunters. It was a community of people who would have to be called upon to restore the vanishing wildlife on a national scale. Roosevelt was quite clear on that point. Again, his words:

It is foolish to regard proper game-laws as undemocratic, unrepublican. On the contrary, they are essentially in the interests of the people as whole, because it is only through their enactment and enforcement that the people as a whole can preserve the game and can prevent its becoming purely the property of the rich, who are able to create and maintain extensive private preserves. The wealthy man can get hunting anyhow, but the man of small means is dependent solely upon wise and well-executed game-laws for his enjoyment of the sturdy pleasure of the chase.[30]

One of our nation's greatest conservation heroes also wrote about the value of wilderness eighty years before a national Wilderness Act was legislated. In those days the term was applied to wild, undeveloped, uncivilized country. It was those wild places, open to all hunters, that stimulated Roosevelt and drove his passion. At one point he addressed it as follows:

Hunting in the wilderness is of all pastimes the most attractive. Shooting over a private game preserve is of course in no way to be compared to it. The Wilderness hunter must not only show skill in the use of the rifle and address in finding and approaching game, but he must also show the qualities of hardihood, self reliance, and resolution needed for . . . grappling with . . . wild surroundings.[31]

There were many others, like those who founded the Boone and Crockett Club with Roosevelt in 1887. Together they campaigned tirelessly against commercial killing for hide, feather, and wild meat markets—and against special privilege in access to wildlife. For the symbolic power of it, however, my mind's eye sees Roosevelt standing there for us. I imagine him, feet spread wide apart, fists planted firmly on his hips, throwing his head back, and then roaring through a broad, toothy grin: *We are going to do this thing and it is going to be for—we the people!*

Less imaginary were arguments advanced by George Bird Grinnell of *Forest and Stream,* the leading sportsmen's magazine of that period. Grinnell, in an editorial entitled "We the People," advanced the argument that wildlife resources are for the good of all the people. He used language we hear repeated to this day, *"the greatest good to the greatest number."* These words became our conservation cornerstone.[32] Roosevelt and his collaborators were setting the stage for the renaissance of North American wildlife.

In the fall of 1901, Vice President Theodore Roosevelt was hunting in the Adirondacks when he received word of President McKinley's assassination. Roosevelt had been shunted into the role of Vice President by leaders of his political party trying to subdue his vigor for reform. "Look," moaned one Republican boss, "that damned cowboy is president of the United States."[33] That damned cowboy was also a hunter, and his commitment to wildlife went beyond urging others to do good things. Roosevelt's record of direct action became enormous.

As president of the United States, Roosevelt created a national wildlife refuge system and various wildlife reserves and by executive order added more than 100 million acres to the national forest reserve system. The refuge system was created on the federal level, and the example was quickly followed at the state level. The forest reserves were viewed, in part, as sanctuaries of wild land where game animals could recover and repopulate the land.

At the state level, wildlife agencies generally came into existence at this time and delivered wildlife protection through enforcement of conservation laws. Momentum was building, and wildlife agencies and laws spread rapidly through state legislatures as the young nation passed from the nineteenth into the twentieth century. The nation needed the laws, the land base, and the protected areas to build upon. What it needed more was the populist notion that if we were going to revive the corpse of North American wildlife, it was going to be by the people and for . . . we the people. That democratic truth was already in our law. The U.S. Supreme Court put it there in 1842 when they ruled that oysters in the New Jersey meadowlands belong to the people. Now Roosevelt, with his words and example, put the fire of it into our hearts.

The stage was set: we had the law, we had inspiration, and we had tasted conservation leadership. All the North American wildlife conservation movement needed to ignite it was a challenge big enough and universal enough to rally an entire nation. Within a generation of Theodore Roosevelt's presidency, our growing nation endured a great economic depression and experienced the drought and dust bowl years of the 1930s, the "dirty thirties." Things were tough all across North America, but from those hard times a new generation of equally tough conservationist hunters was about to emerge.

THE HUNTER'S GOLDEN AGE

For wildlife, the "dirty thirties" satisfied the cliché that it was always darkest just before the dawn. Writer Lonnie Williamson summarized the times:

> Drought, panic and poverty spread across . . . America as the 1930s arrived. Bone-dry winds and economic depression combined to break institutions, families and spirits. The dust storms and unemployment whipped wildlife habitat destruction and poaching to a peak. People were hungry, ammunition was inexpensive, and game provided high-quality protein. Waterfowl hit all-time lows. Other wildlife populations began to falter also. Gains that had been made in wildlife restoration since the century's turn began to erode.[34]

From this seedbed of despair a generation of new giants grew to capture the truth of Theodore Roosevelt's populist vision for wildlife of the North American commons. When Theodore Roosevelt's vision was coupled to Franklin Roosevelt's generation of New Deal conservation initiatives, good things began to happen. The new wildlife advocates came from all walks of life, from across the political spectrum, from the media, from the universities, from the conservation agencies, and from farms, cities, and towns all across North America. These advocates worked with government and within government, and when necessary, they created private organizations to address wildlife's needs. Their names and deeds fill the volumes of our history; their achievements filled the habitats of North America.

Like Theodore Roosevelt, for the most part these conservation activists were hunters. Today their achievements live in the grizzly of the Northern Rockies, the elk of Wyoming and Colorado, the white-tailed deer and wild turkey of New Jersey, Kansas, Tennessee, Oklahoma, Wisconsin, Pennsylvania, and, well, everywhere. Wildlife, wetlands, a wonderful wilderness system, and humble pockets of wildness in every corner of the continent became their legacy. All of these things are now our heritage by virtue of our citizenship.

In the middle of that dirty decade turning golden, the kid who shot the sparrow was born. It is difficult to claim the year of my birth was a good year. Hitler had just renounced the treaty of Versailles, Italy had invaded Ethiopia, the Great Plains were blowing eastward, Huey Long was assassinated in the Louisiana capitol building, and one of the nation's most popular songs was "I Got Plenty of Nothin." On a more positive note, Aldo Leopold visited his shack on the Wisconsin River for the first time, and it was the year he and others founded The Wilderness Society.

In a curious alignment of events, the year I was born in Wisconsin, hunters in Montana formed their first statewide wildlife conservation association. When they did, 10,000 pronghorn antelope were scattered over Montana's eastern plains. Nineteen years later, when I hunted antelope in Montana for the first time, five times that many antelope lived on that same prairie habitat. Since then, the antelope population has grown beyond 100,000. I shot a beautiful young buck on my first pronghorn hunt in the fall of 1954. At the time I knew nothing of those people and what they had done so that the animals would be there when I found my way to Montana's prairie grasslands.

When I was one year old, seven Montana conservationists went to Washington, D.C., to help form a national citizen's organization for wildlife. Others came from state wildlife conservation organizations of the

West Coast, the Lake States, the Heartland, the South, the Southwest, and New England. They assembled from all across the nation because the people—all the people—cared. From that grassroots assemblage of citizen hunters, a populist conservation energy blossomed. A great federation, the National Wildlife Federation, took shape, and it formed with a purpose, the restoration of wildlife for all of us.

❧❧❧

Because I owe these people a lot, I pause to name the Montana emissaries to that historic event. They deserve to be remembered, remembered by me and all hunters who take liberally of their fruit. They were: L.W. Wendt, Ray G. Lowe, B.L. Price, M.A. Malone, Emil Knoepke, Glen Smith, and Kenneth McDonald. Of these seven, three were involved either professionally or politically with the wildlife resource. One was a state fish and game commissioner, one a national forest supervisor, and one a game warden. All were hunters.[35]

❦❦❦

The beauty of this golden age of mid-century was the unity of purpose, the unity of effort, and the pride taken in common cause. The goal was clear: restore and conserve wildlife, and do it for all the people. We all work, we all enjoy, and we all share: professional and lay conservationist, landowner and hunter, firearm and ammunition manufacturers and license buyer—everyone—together.

After the delegates returned from Washington, the Montana group organized the Montana Wildlife Federation. At the state federation's first meeting in May 1936 they were addressed by a Crow Indian Chief, Robert Yellowtail, who told them:

> Wildlife in America is disappearing so fast the Osages in Oklahoma now pay $1 for a squirrel or rabbit and consider it a game dinner. There is need for concerted action to save the buffalo and other big game of the west.[36]

The National Wildlife Federation, with Iowa's Jay Norwood "Ding" Darling at the helm, went immediately to work on creative conservation legislation. It didn't take long for things to start happening. In 1937, the U.S. Congress passed, and the President signed, the law that ignited the wildlife recovery process, the Wildlife Restoration Act, more commonly known as the Pittman-Robertson (PR) Act. The hunting industry had stepped up in support of this federal excise tax on firearms and ammunition, and the states quickly tied their hunting license revenue to wildlife programs to qualify for the new federal funds. Together these steps were the golden touch for the golden age of restoration. The law was a stroke of genius, its design was flawless, and it became the Midas of wildlife's future.

The chief architect of this law was Carl Shoemaker, an attorney from Ohio who also had a distinguished career as an Oregon conservationist before moving to Washington, D.C. The legislation's congressional sponsors were Senator Key Pittman of Nevada and Representative A. Willis Robertson of Virginia. The stroke of genius came when Pittman designed language requiring all state hunting license revenues be kept within the wildlife program. This ended the practice of diverting license revenues into other needs such as roads and schools, and it meant millions of dollars for wildlife through the years.

From the beginning of the campaign to pass this critical legislation, the shooting industries whose products were to be taxed stepped forward in *support* of the idea. The progressive corporations included DuPont, Federal Cartridge, and Remington Arms.

The achievements of the PR Act became enormous. Ever since the turn of the century, state wildlife agencies had concentrated on game laws and law enforcement programs. It was the most direct approach to the protection of fish and game. To broaden state wildlife programs, the PR money was channeled into wildlife research, management, land acquisition, and, later, hunter education. State wildlife law enforcement programs remained funded by license revenue. Under this traditional funding structure, state game wardens were performing some truly heroic acts. Their deeds made a statement about how law enforcement people viewed their role in the business of protecting the people's game.

Some wildlife populations had problems beyond the reach of state and federal programs, such as the need to preserve international wetlands for migratory waterfowl. Hunters once again stepped forward, in essence taxing themselves by forming fundraising conservation groups to address the problem. In the same year Congress passed the PR Act, Ducks Unlimited (DU) was founded in the private sector to raise money to protect and restore wetland habitat. In 1997, when DU passed its 60th anniversary, it had more than 604,000 members. When DU passed that six-decade checkpoint, it had created more than 7.5 million acres of wetlands and preserved more than 15,000 miles of waterfowl nesting shoreline.[37]

All across the continent, effective law enforcement, habitat protection, and a growing sophistication in wildlife management replenished the depleted habitats of North America. The hunters had learned the value of protection, the value of production, the value of management, and the value of sharing. The years stretched into decades, the progress in wildlife restoration continued, and, almost without notice, one generation replaced another and now—still another.

The new generations of hunters and non-hunters never knew, and most were never told, about the hard times. The Wisconsin county of my birth, nearly barren of game fish and wildlife in my youth, now supplies deer, salmon, and grouse to my brother's children—and no one told them. Kansas, the state that "had no deer" in my adolescent recollection, is now rich in white-tailed deer, wild turkey, pheasants, and more. When Chief Yellowtail offered comment on the sad state of wildlife to the Montana Wildlife Federation in 1936, he used the plight of the Oklahoma Osage Indians as an example. In 1940, the entire deer harvest in Oklahoma was 318 deer. Today, Oklahoma's wildlife management program is strong enough to sustain a harvest in the vicinity of 50,000 deer, every year.

John Phillips, the deer hunter who feared he had killed the last deer in Pennsylvania, can now rest peacefully. Today, Pennsylvania is again one of the great hunting states in North America, sustaining an annual harvest of nearly 400,000 deer.

It is also important to look back to New Jersey to measure the wisdom of endowing the public with the responsibility for wildlife. It was in that state that the argument over public access to the oysters of the meadowlands eventually led to endowing all the people with access to fish and wildlife as well as the trust for their management. New Jersey has kept records of deer harvest since 1905, when Theodore Roosevelt happened to be in the White House. The highest deer harvests on record are being achieved now, in the 1990s. In 1995, more than 100,000 hunters went afield in New Jersey, and 58,000 came home with venison, a level of success carefully nurtured.

When the sparrow hunter went west in his eighteenth year, the formula for democratic access to wildlife and citizen conservation of wildlife had already restored the western ranges with wildlife, and my dreaming was fulfilled. Forty years later, when I look back to the depleted fields of my youth, to where the little bird had died a generation ago, there is a new generation of hunters, and they too are living with the new abundance. My brother and his family dine on white-tailed deer his children bring home from the reclaimed Kettle Moraine Forest and on steelhead trout that found their way back up the Pigeon River. The stories go on, but the point is the same. Wherever the environment is not overrun by civilization, hunters, landowners, and wildlife managers are sustaining a precious value: *wildness and the wildlife it can sustain,* all across North America.

A Game Warden for the People's Fish

The dedication and just plain heroism displayed by game wardens went far beyond what the gamekeepers of Old England might be expected to risk to protect the king's deer. The core of that courage almost certainly flowed from a sense of patriotism associated with protecting something that belonged to free people in a democratic society. No story makes the point better than author Jim Chizek's story, The Saga of Ernie Swift.[38]

The story is set in Wisconsin's "up north," an area missing out on the glitter of the "Roaring Twenties" while enduring the effects of prohibition. The late 1920s were tough times, and this was a tough place. Wisconsin folks spoke of the road through it as "the road to Hayward, Hurley, and Hell!" What made it extremely nasty and dangerous was the fact that prohibition-era mobsters used the area as a cooling off retreat when things got too hot in Chicago. The area also happened to have some pretty good fishing spots. To maintain the fishery, the state had established a 2,000-foot no-fishing section below Winter Dam on the Chippewa River to protect spawning walleye and other game fish concentrated there. Author Chizek describes the cast of characters who occasionally hung out in the Wisconsin woods:

The notorious Al Capone had a retreat . . . aptly named the Hideaway Resort. Other well-known mobsters habituating the area was the Moran and Touhy gang, the Joe Saltis gang of which Frank McErlane known as Machine Gun Frankie, inventor of the one-way ride, Stanley Novak and Tony Maloga were members, the deadly Barker Karpes gang, Potatoes Koffman, Lefty Koncel, Gus Winkler and many others.

These people had a lot of bad habits, and fishing in the refuge was one of them. They were some of the meanest killers in the history of crime, always heavily armed and contemptuous of any law enforcement. Time and again, Wisconsin game warden Ernie Swift busted them. Sometimes he took them down with help and sometimes he went alone. They were the people's fish, the state had ordered them protected, and the people's interest was represented by warden Swift. It is hard to imagine that kind of risk and that level of courage coming from any source other than a sense of patriotism in an institution belonging to all the people in the land of the free and, in this case certainly, the home of the brave.

Warden Ernie Swift went on to an illustrious conservation career that included service as director of the Wisconsin Conservation Department and, later, executive director of the National Wildlife Federation. His adversaries of that generally lawless era also went on—most likely to the last stop on the road through Hayward, Hurley, and Hell. The lesson Swift left us with, however, is that the highest level of public service comes from standing tall in defense of things that belong to "we the people." The Sheriff of Nottingham stayed out of Sherwood Forest, but Ernie Swift went to the banks of the Chippewa River and stood there, tall—for all of us.

Establishing the public interest in fish and wildlife in the nineteenth century; vitalizing the concept that it was for all the people early in the twentieth century; and energizing fish and wildlife restoration programs by the middle of that century, worked miracles on the land.

❧❧❧

The next plateau in this saga is nurturing *a hunting ethic* capable of sustaining hunting in a society growing distant from nature, natural rhythms, and the beauty of an honest association with wildness.

THE ESCUDILLA
AND OUR HUNTING ETHIC

Aldo Leopold was a two-year-old in Iowa when Theodore Roosevelt shot one of the last wild buffalo in Idaho and the Sioux were dancing the Ghost Dance in South Dakota. Later, as the twentieth century approached its mid-point, Leopold died fighting a grass fire near the farmstead he had nurtured back to health. The fruit of Leopold's legacy, like his farm, are still full of life and relevance. He left us a rich collection of papers, essays, and a book, *A Sand County Almanac,* to give us guidance, stimulate our thinking, and measure our progress. In this good book, Leopold defined the land ethic as follows:

> A thing is right when it tends to preserve the integrity, stability, and beauty of a biotic community. It is wrong when it tends otherwise.[39]

North American hunters, as a community of hunters, certainly have a collective ethic that fulfills this definition. It resides with those 100,000 antelope restored to Montana's high plains and the deer in

Kansas, Oklahoma, New Jersey,and every other state and province in North America. It is a success story restrained only by the limits of what the animals find suitable. This collective ethic lives with four million wild turkeys now back from the brink of extinction. The collective ethic lies along the 15,000 miles of nesting shoreline the duck hunters took under their wing. These are not the accomplishments of one person; rather they are a collective hunter ethic achieved by thousands of individual acts of farmers, ranchers, hunters, hunter organizations, agencies supported by hunters, and the general public. It could have happened no other way.

The American Southwest where Aldo Leopold worked as a young forester inspired one of his most important essays. It is about a mountain, Escudilla, that has watched many generations and a few civilizations pass across its face. A story about recent events on that same landscape demonstrates the nature of the land ethic still robustly alive in the hunting community.

Escudilla Revisited

In 1994, I traveled with others across the hot desert between Albuquerque, New Mexico, and Springerville,

Arizona. Our purpose was to celebrate a small part of the hunters' ethic, the making of land whole again. We were on our way to the same ground that Aldo Leopold walked eight decades before. This was the country that was so important in honing his perceptions and crystallizing his philosophy. It was the place where Leopold found the inspiration for his classic essay, "Thinking like a Mountain." The essay is an articulation of ideas and perceptions so strong and durable that they have inspired three generations of wildlife conservationists, while they grow stronger with time. Of that country Leopold wrote:

> Life in Arizona was bounded under foot by grama grass, overhead by sky, and on the horizon by Escudilla. To the north of the mountain you rode on honey colored plains. Look up anywhere, any time, and you saw—Escudilla.[40]

Leopold's season in the Southwest was spent with the last grizzlies and wolves clinging to what was then a withering, wild place. The land's wildness was grudgingly giving ground to civilization. Somewhere in the mountains we passed through, Leopold had heard wolves, and he remembered the sound with clarity. Later he wrote about the "deep chesty bawl" that echoed from the rimrocks. He described it as a "wild defiant sorrow, and contempt for . . . the adversities of the world." Leopold watched that wildness fade as a she-wolf he shot died. The sight of that "fierce green fire dying in her eyes" was burned forever on his soul.

The story about the death of one of the region's last wolves unfolded in the Blue River country not far south of Escudilla. It is possible to imagine that on a still morning, across that high plateau country, a fading echo of that distant shot reached the silent face of Escudilla. We do know Old Bigfoot, the last grizzly to pad those juniper ridges, ponderosa pine slopes, and cottonwood creek bottoms called that big mountain his own. It was on the shoulders of that towering mass that the government trapper's set gun killed Arizona's last grizzly. We also know the hide brought down from the mountain was big enough to tax the strength of a mule and there was only one barn in town big enough to dry it on.

On July 10, 1994, two generations later, we gathered to dedicate a special piece of ground and to celebrate what the people had achieved. There was an important change at hand. More than a thousand acres of critical wildlife habitat had just been acquired. The acquisition guaranteed the future of a threatened fish, waterfowl-rich wetlands, a rare willow, and up to one thousand elk that seek the bottomlands for winter survival. The people were mostly members of the Rocky Mountain Elk Foundation. They had volunteered their time and had given of their financial and human resources so that the elk they hunt might prosper. On Friday they had repaired a barn, on Saturday they hosted a barbecue, and on Sunday they took a seat in the shade to hear words spoken to dedicate their achievement.

One by one, speakers took the podium to say what was proper and to note the human attributes necessary to make good things happen in a complex world. Note was taken of the institutions created to preserve what we value. Recognition was afforded to Arizona's Heritage Fund and Lottery, Waterfowl Conservation Funds, and those still reliable Pittman-Robertson Wildlife Restoration Funds. In proper order, note was taken of the private landowner, Arizona's Game and Fish officials, and the effort of the staff and volunteers of the Rocky Mountain Elk Foundation. One by one, speakers shared what was in their hearts, and it had to do with wildlife, the future, and another generation to share the legacy.

The folks gathered to listen sat in chairs placed in the shelter of a grove of cottonwood trees. A soft breeze fluttered the leaves, softening the mid-day heat. From the seats it was impossible not to let the eye wander beyond the speaker's platform, out across the adjacent meadow, then up over the near ridge, and there it was— *Escudilla.* The mountain was just there—brooding like a huge blue shadow, shimmering through the mid-day heat. As I stared at the mountain, I realized something exceptional was happening on that sun-baked Arizona field.

Dedications are important events. Here, however, within the reach of Escudilla, the ceremony took on an almost spiritual dimension. The mountain was there, holding the memory of that enormous grizzly. The echo of the wolf's howl was buried in that mountain. The magic that touched the heart and ignited the mind of the young Leopold so long ago was still up on those slopes. This mountain easily captured what was being said, just as it caught and held the faint echo of Leopold's shot, and the crack of the rifle that felled the great bear. Looking at the mountain it became clear that the hunters of Arizona had indeed done something important, not only for themselves, but for every hunter in North America. Leopold, the hunter's mentor, learned from that mountain and then he told us:

> A thing is right when it tends to preserve the integrity, stability, and beauty of a biotic community. It is wrong when it tends otherwise.

The hunters of Arizona and the people they rallied were doing what was right. They were preserving the integrity, stability, and beauty of this biotic community. They fulfilled the promise ethical hunters make to the animals and to the land; it was a commitment fulfilled to the elk, to the tiny fish in trouble, to our sons and daughters, and to a great brooding mountain.

I only spent a couple of days with those people and saw no evidence that any of them knew Leopold's definition. Yet, they did something almost holy. They restored some wildness to a mountain that had inspired our most perceptive teacher. These people accomplished what the legions of academics and scholars who recite Leopold's words with great redundancy and accuracy generally fail to actually do. The Arizona hunters touched the earth and made it better. These people had walked on the mountain the same way the young Leopold did, with a rifle in hand. They had gone to the mountain just as Leopold had, and they had learned. What Leopold so beautifully articulated, they, just as beautifully, had now fulfilled.

In the fall of 1994, as in every fall, hunters returned to the breast of Escudilla. They went to hunt elk, turkey, and deer. They were and are the hunting community's emissaries to the great mountain. In the fall of 1994 they told Escudilla that we heard the lessons of Leopold, that we have taken care of the elk, the ducks, the tiny fish, and the rare willow. Most of all, they told Escudilla for all of us: the green fire of wildness did not die with Leopold's she-wolf. The hunter kept the fire alive until she could return.

Early in 1998, following an absence of nearly half a century, wolves were reintroduced in the Blue Range Recovery Area of Arizona and New Mexico. That spring the first wolf pup was born in the wild.

LESSONS FROM THE VIENNA WOODS, THE KYRGY PLAIN, AND THE AMERICAN COMMONS

About a decade before my trip to Arizona and the mountain Escudilla, I attended a convention in Vienna, Austria. When it ended I stayed to walk in the Vienna Woods, appreciate Austrian decors rich in artistic symbols of hunting, enjoy music in Vienna's city parks, relish schnitzels, and savor beer. Public transport and the Austrian trail system were beautifully coordinated, so getting around was easy. Leaving behind the perceptions and values of a fish and wildlife advocate, however, was no longer possible; they had become too much a part of me.

Morning walks along the concrete-lined canals and cement flumes carrying water through Vienna were void of any natural aesthetic. Some local people were seen fishing each morning in the canals. A fish like a sucker appeared to be the prize. No one fished for anything in the concrete flumes that had once been streams.

Memories of Montana in the early sixties were vivid

in my mind. It was a time when anglers and civic groups, such as the Montana Junior Chamber of Commerce, forged into law a stream preservation act that forbid the physical manipulation and paving of natural waterways. What I saw in Vienna would have been a crime in a country where anglers were numerous, had the right to cast for trout, and had, for two centuries, the right to cast a vote.

A name on the map, *Lanizer Tier Garten,* caught my attention, and I caught the trolley, transferred to the U-Bahn (subway), and then to a bus to find my way to this Lanizer animal park. The place was once the royal hunting ground. I found it surrounded by a high, yellow wall. Entering through a small gateway, I passed instantly into a hardwood forest. It was a curious transformation, like passing back through time rather than just through a turnstile that granted admission. Inside, it was quiet and peaceful. The wall and trees muted the traffic noise, and I could hear the breeze moving through the thick overstory.

The forest was cool. The dark forest canopy contrasted sharply with the bright, sunny meadows scattered throughout the area. It was a beautiful place, and true to the culture, a rustic gasthaus near its center offered lunch and libation to the hiker. Behind the gasthaus, near the edge of a thicket, a trough for garbage was tucked in the shade. Its purpose was to lure wild boar within view of the resting and dining hikers. I remembered the successful fight to close an open dump on the edge of a small tourist town near Yellowstone National Park. There, bears lured by garbage had entertained tourists for years. The predictable and universal nature of bears, boars, and humans is a marvel.

The gasthaus was beautifully appointed with icons of the hunt. Tusks of boar, antlers of roebuck, bleached skull plates with the antlers of red and fallow deer, mounted grouse, and polished hunting horns were artfully displayed on the bright white walls and dark, rough-hewn beams. While walking through the forest, I had noticed shooting stands strategically placed to overlook the meadows and forest edge. It was clear that this was a well-managed and active shooting ground for a few Austrians. I imagined them with their beautiful, artistically engraved, classic firearms. It was easy to visualize them taking their place in the elaborate shooting stands, dressed for the hunt in loden coats or capes and green Tyrolian hats. True to the European tradition each animal shot from the high seats would be honored with respectful ritual and then utilized.

There are still places on the European continent where the land is wilder than this remnant of the Austrian forest I visited. There are also many rich and admirable European hunting traditions. The animal is always honored and respected in solemn ritual. The hunters are trained, competent, and held in high regard in their communities. Still, something is missing. Perhaps Leopold described it in 1933 when he gave this counsel in the first comprehensive text on wildlife management written in North America:

> The . . . value of game is inverse to the artificiality of its origin, and hence . . . to the degree of control exercised in its production.[41]

There was a lot of control exercised inside the yellow wall, and somehow the classic firearms, elaborate ceremony, and beautiful traditions failed to completely fill the void. The whole thing was . . . hollow. Now, in retrospect, I think I was looking at the end of the trail. This is where the royals and people of privilege had taken hunting. There never was an evil intent, but the outcome had been inevitable. The European hunting culture excluded most of the common people. On the outside, beyond the wall, there was a whole nation, possibly resentful or more likely not really interested in wildlife, its abundance, or the means of its demise.

Now, almost a quarter century after having visited that place, I think I finally recognize what I had witnessed behind the wall. It was the European hunter's equivalent of a ghost dance. One of the most beautiful regions on earth had simply crushed its wild places with other necessities. This was a patch of forest, at one time suitable for a handful of royal hunters. It was a hunting ground passed through the centuries to people of means or privilege, people who dress in the uniform of the hunt, shoot carefully kept animals, and perform a solemn ritual. It is, however, a ritual conducted with animals held captive and with shooters generations removed from the fair-chase pursuit of game through a wild land. The shooting behind the wall will not bring back the wildness that once was alive in this part of Europe. It will not bring back the hunt for very many ordinary Austrian boys or girls born with a hunter's desire embedded in their genetic code.

❧❧❧

In July of 1994 I again traveled to the Old World. This time the destination was the Central Asian republic of Kyrgyzstan, one of the nations granted independence with the breakup of the old Soviet Union. The travel schedule included a few days in Germany. The layover was spent meeting conservationists in Frankfurt, touring a wildcat reintroduction project in the Spessart Forest, dining on wild boar at Gasthaus im Hochspessart, and coping with jet lag.

The visit to the wildcat reintroduction project was encouraging. The letdown came when the forester told me that hunting rights on the state forest sold for 70,000 D-Marks. A German corporation bought them. It was a matter-of-fact statement made without a second thought about how these things were done. They were done, as they had always been done. If you had the money you can buy the right to hunt. No one could remember it any other way. The German forest is managed with obvious competence and pride. It was clearly a more wild place than the Austrian park. Hunters, however, came to the state forest only by invitation from the corporation that purchased the hunting rights.

Kyrgyzstan was a ten-hour flight east from Frankfurt, with a mid-course adjustment just west of Moscow. It was a markedly different place, yet its relevance to those of us who hunt was remarkably the same. Now a republic, Kyrgyzstan is about the size of South Dakota. Forty percent of the country is more than 9,000 feet above sea level. The remote wild land, the *Tien Shan* (Sky Mountains), is the northern extension of the Tibetan Plateau. The nation's high ground, Pobeda Peak, passes spectacularly through 24,000 feet. It is a land where horses are known as "man's wind," where horse milk, *cummis,* is the beverage of choice (theirs), and a national sport, *Ulak tartysh,* involves teams of magnificent horsemen wrestling for possession of a beheaded goat. It is a land of vast intermountain valleys under a crystalline sky—a land without fences, a sky without contrails.

Here on the edge of the Sky Mountains there is an overpowering sweep of wild country. There were no walled-in ancient hunting grounds. In fact, in our extensive travel we never encountered a fence. Each morning and each evening I walked on the grassy plains or wandered the foothills of immense intermountain valleys. From prominent points I searched the dawn and evening landscapes for whatever antelope might have been native to those sweeping plains. I scanned the slopes of bordering mountain ranges for the red deer whose concrete statue I had noted along the highway *en route* to the remote places. Not once was anything sighted. My mind returned to frequent trips I have made between Sheridan and Sundance, Wyoming, where for more than a hundred miles antelope are almost never out of sight from the interstate highway, at any time of day.

In Kyrgyzstan, the animals of the hunt are the Marco Polo sheep and the ibex. These animals live in some of the most rugged and remote country on earth. They survive beyond the terrain that can be grazed with domestic animals, which is one of two reasons they exist at all. Because the country is in need of economic activity, a new kind of royalty is imported to hunt them. In 1994, a Marco Polo hunt cost $35,000, which buys the hunter government guides and three cartridges. You are expected to be a competent shooter. This is a country that needs capital, and hunting brings in a little. That is the second reason the sheep and ibex still exist.

I was traveling with a handful of German "greens" and a small group of European journalists. The greens are Europe's more dedicated environmental activists, and most on this excursion carried an anti-hunting bias.

Their environmental movement did not grow from hunter/conservationists as it did in North America. The Marco Polo hunt was the source of constant debate among us. People on both sides of the debate could and did exaggerate, perhaps they even told a few untruths when arguing for or against hunting. The truth of the matter was, however, to bring the money, there must be massive rams in the sheep population.

The debate about hunting eventually focused on the sheep themselves, and the fact that they, the sheep, could not lie. They either exist or they don't. Big rams cannot be imagined or bribed into a wild population. If the wild mountains of Kyrgyzstan are to have big old rams, the entire sheep population pyramid that produces them must be nurtured. There is no other way. You can't have big rams without sub-adult rams and even more ewes and lambs supporting them. To end the hunt would be to deny the incentive that holds the population pyramid together. I found depending on the flow of money as a basis for conservation a distasteful argument, but I used it to prevail. I know that as soon as something more lucrative comes along, the sheep will be abandoned. Chances are good that there would be no public protest. I was too far from home to try and impose a more reliable philosophy and value system for saving wild sheep. I was just passing through.

❦❦❦

Western Europe and Kyrgyzstan are very different places with a common tragedy. The wildlife commons does not exist in either of them. Should children there aspire to be hunters, it will probably be an unfulfilled aspiration. In Austria, the wildness was lost to the crush of civilization, and game animals are simply someone's property. In Germany, it is similar, even on the state forest. When a more lucrative use for the property comes along, the decision will be relatively simple. In the meantime, even the ritual of the hunt is acted out by a very few. In Kyrgyzstan, the native people have fashioned an existence totally dependent on domestic animals. It is a way of life that has existed for thousands of years. The hunt, a government-run commercial operation, occurs only in the deepest pockets of ruggedly wild, mountain terrain. The hunt will persist until something of higher commercial value comes along.

Each of these trips to the Old World was relevant to understanding and appreciating the importance of hunting and hunters in North America. The modern North American hunting tradition is distinctly remarkable. It is a tradition with common people endowed with an individual human right to be a hunter, if they choose. It is a heritage in which the animals are wild and free, and their interest is held in common by the people. The people's wildlife are not economic commodities.

The trail of events that brought these truths to our time began a very long time ago. It included Stone Age mammoth hunters, early Roman law, English barons and common law, colonial charters, and, finally, American patriots who declared our land, the wildlife, and we the people—free.

FINDING OUR WAY
IN THE TWENTY-FIRST
CENTURY

When I shot that sparrow as a youth, I found the hunter's trail and followed it through life. Later it became a track I followed in reverse, making a pilgrimage through history, looking for the reasons why I could be a hunter, and why, on this continent, anyone could be a hunter. On its trail through time, our hunting heritage crossed some scary ground. It was a trail that almost disappeared into the black oblivion of extinction during wildlife's dark age of commercial killing. It was a trail born again and blazed fresh in the words of Theodore Roosevelt, the thoughts of Aldo Leopold, the courage of Ernie Swift, and the deeds of the several generations of hunters who filled our fields, forests, and lives with wildlife.

The common citizen, blue-collar, we-the-people hunters of North America now approach the transition from the twentieth to the twenty-first century. With our fields rich with game, there is a future to be fashioned from our choices. We address that future in a social environment where hunting is challenged by some, coveted by others, and hoarded by a few. The market for hides and meat has been replaced by a new commerce. It is commerce of gadgets, hunting machinery, catered experiences, and fees for access to what is ours. We address our future with some wildlife agencies and public land managers estranged from hunters and unaware of the important public trust we placed in them.

These challenges before our generation are as substantial as those confronted by the generation that won our liberty, by the generation that established our public wildlife trust, and by those who returned game animals to abundance. We face these challenges armed with the truth of our own history, the wisdom born of experience, and the power that democracy gives its citizens.

When game animals were scarce or absent, few challenged the hunt, or the hunters, as they stepped forward as conservationists. The bystanders offered praise as hunter/conservationists shut down the commercial killing, extended protection to game animals, financed management agencies, restored wetlands, and stood in defense of the earth. When it came time to protect the fading wilderness, the idea for its preservation found its birth around the hunter's fire. Many national, regional, and local environmental organizations drew their energy from the traditional conservation ethic of hunters and their organizations. The pedestal of honor truly belonged to the hunter.

New generations replace the old subtly, and we face the new millennium with new people. Among them are hunters who never knew wildlife's bad times and know little of their own history. Access to hunting opportunity is critical, yet there are some among us who engage in practices of exclusion to give advantage to themselves. The society we are part of consists of a significant majority who do not hunt, are unaware of the hunter's history, and unappreciative of the wildlife renaissance crafted by hunters.

Hunting's survival in our democracy will be decided by people who are neither for nor against hunting. If there is freedom in truth, our liberation from the aggravation of anti-hunters will come as we revive and teach the historical reality of the hunter's heritage, and carry that reality to the whole community. The anti-hunting notion that wildlife will flourish when human hunters are retired from all natural communities is a myth that can only flourish where the truth of history is ignored or denied. Hunters can free themselves from this irritation by embracing, and then extending, the conservation ethic of our predecessors. When the public sees us as hunters and as custodians of wildlife, the pedestal of social acceptability will be ours, and hunting will be secure.

There are more serious threats to hunting than a handful of anti-hunters making a living off their advocacy. The most ominous threat is carried by those who would create the equivalent of a new royalty of the hunt in North America. It is critical that *anyone* who hunts see himself or herself in the context of *everyone* who hunts, or who would some day hunt. We must all choose to see ourselves as members of the larger community. It took people from all segments of our society to put the wildlife resource back on the land, and for that resource to be sustained, *it must be shared.* To be true to our heritage we must reject the notion of securing advantages in the hunt by denying opportunity to others. If we have a cancer within our collective body, this is it. The symptoms of the malady are: making money the dominant criteria for access to this public resource, implying that killing is hunting success, and allowing public trustees to pander to the commerce of hunting at the expense of the public interest.

Theodore Roosevelt was a Harvard-educated man of considerable personal wealth. He and others of his time could easily have adopted an elitist attitude and simply acquired privilege. Roosevelt, George Bird Grinnell, and their associates, however, used their considerable power not to separate themselves from the less advantaged, but to champion a common cause. There was a higher form of nobility in these people, a nobility void of any notion of class distinction. Again, the unmistakable bare-knuckle power of Roosevelt's words:

> The professional market hunter who kills game for the hide or for the feathers or for the meat or to sell antlers and other trophies; market men who put game in cold storage; and the rich people, who are content to buy what they have not the skill to get by their own exertions—these are the men who are the real enemies of game.[42]

It is time for hunters, landowners, wildlife managers, and the public trustees to gather around the hunter's fire. It is time to once again look at our movement's compass and contemplate both our direction and future. We have been drifting into a system of wildlife management that advantages commerce, tolerates exclusion, and creates a class system within the North American hunting community. We cannot profess to be advocates of the hunting heritage and engage in these practices. Creating exclusive hunting areas where participants are taken to a shooting ground and told they are hunters is the antithesis of Roosevelt's notion of gaining honor through effort. At their worst, these activities represent illusions of hunting, another ghost dance of the hunt.

The threat to our future as hunters is compounded when public trustees yield to the concentrated influence of the minorities seeking privileged access to public resources. Our "golden age" of wildlife was built on a common purpose pursued by state wildlife agencies and hunters. The partnership was strengthened by a system of state wildlife commissions patterned after a law pioneered in the 1930s by "Ding" Darling of Iowa, Syd Stephens of Missouri, and the National Wildlife Federation. The law moderated political influences that were compromising the vigor of wildlife conservation agencies.[43] It was a way of managing wild resources that had no access to ballot boxes, and it functioned well for wildlife and the public interest. It is a system, however,

that has deteriorated in so many states that, in 1993, the
State Wildlife Laws Handbook carried the conclusion
that:

> Many states have bestowed the authority on the
> governor to appoint the fish and wildlife . . . direc-
> tors and commissioners, who . . . serve at the
> pleasure of the governor . . . This can lead to a
> politicized commission and department . . .[44]

Thus, it is no surprise when the allocation of hunting opportunity takes on a design to favor minority
interests that have influence, when hunting permits are
sold to the highest bidder, and when commercial interests are given privilege. These actions undermine the
principle of equal opportunity and equal treatment fun-
damental to our democracy and the public interest in
wildlife. These actions create a privileged group and
dredge up the decaying residuals of a class system.
These actions violate the public trust responsibilities
invested in our wildlife agencies. The tragedy is compounded in a few places where public bodies with the
trust responsibility to preserve the democracy of hunting become willing participants in its demise. We must

never forget the images of a class system that still torment what little hunting remains in England, a torment
that has lasted for thirteen centuries.

Threats to the future of hunting in North America
are real. However, the serious perils do not come from
those who assail hunting, but from those who try to
possess or exploit what belongs to all of us. We all need
to remember that poaching was honorable when royalty controlled access to deer and denied access to the
people. Should game animals become the property of
some kind of "new royalty," we will have seen our last
courageous enforcer in the mold of Ernie Swift. Should
that happen, each of us can retire to our last hidden
sanctuary and perform our own last ritual to the notion
of hunting opportunity for all people free and equal
before God and each other.

North American hunters have other issues to
address as we extend our heritage into the new century.
Again, our predecessors showed the way, and history
has judged their aim to be true. The trail they followed
was hard, but the tracks are clear. In 1997, I attended
the Rocky Mountain Elk Foundation's Eastern
Rendezvous at King of Prussia, Pennsylvania. The convention hotel was within sight of Valley Forge. I walked

those hills on a cold misty January afternoon and stood by the marker noting where the Massachusetts Infantry camped for a winter. My thoughts were of those men who validated the Declaration of Independence. It was that declaration that the U.S. Supreme Court used to declare our equality, our sovereignty, and our right to gather from the commons. Our chance to be hunters was among those opportunities. The men camped on those hills paid an awesome price before they emerged from their hour of darkness to win our liberty.

Later that same year, I was in Tennessee to work with hunter educators. While there, the magazine *Tennessee Conservationist* reminded me of the volunteer freedom fighters known as the "over-the-mountain men" who assembled at Sycamore Shoals, Tennessee, and then came to the aid of the revolutionary fighters. Had all these various people not stepped forward to prevail, the King of England's grant of "the fishings, huntings . . . and fowlings" as the private property of the Duke of York might have endured.

The descendants of those heroic revolutionary fighters are now being denied access to the hunt because of excessive demands for money. For example, if they choose to hunt in almost any western state, it is big money for non-resident licenses, money for services, and in some cases still more money for access. Exclusion based solely on wealth is no way to share a heritage built on democratic principles and common sacrifice.

We are participants in the great drama of life, and our stage is the land. Decisions made by private landowners have always been a major influence on how wildlife prospers and on how it is shared among the people. All across North America the pattern of land ownership and the philosophy of those who manage the private estate is changing. The days when rural landowners were engaged exclusively in agrarian enterprises are passing into history. The old pattern of ownership was crucial in wildlife's recovery, and many farmers and ranchers clearly understood, practiced, and enjoyed what Leopold called the "pleasures of husbandry-in-the-wild." Those who appreciated wildlife made concessions to the animals and shared the result because they were neighbors, they were the land stewards of the conservation community, and often they were hunters—just like us.

Those traditional landowners are now blended with urban people owning rural land in tracts ranging from cozy wood lots to sprawling western estates. These lifestyle choices generally include an appreciation for the presence of wildlife. We cannot assume, however, that the ethic of these new landowners includes an understanding of how wildlife was restored through common effort of the whole community. The new people will be staying. Many of them understand and practice the principle of *noblesse oblige* (the moral obligation of the advantaged to display honorable or charitable conduct), and some come with the same motivation that brought Theodore Roosevelt from New York City to Medora, North Dakota. That may have been the most important move in the history of our heritage. Within the mix of traditional landowners and the new migrants lies the challenge to create a positive relationship. Conservation-oriented landowners and ethical hunters have the potential to take our North American hunting ethic to new ground. We must find one another, search for the common ground, and then find ways to nurture the spirit of Roosevelt's populist hunting ethic both in our hearts and in theirs.

The social issues within our hunting culture and humanity's relentless pressure on the wild places of earth are testing our generation as they have tested no other. But then, there is an instinct within us, as hunters, that enables us to address perils and obstacles when in pursuit of something special. For us, the real reward is an enriched abundance of game and a sustained democracy of the hunt. If we can succeed, we will have indeed claimed a real trophy—the big prize—the heritage preserved.

EPILOGUE

When my desire to hunt put me on this hunter's trail, I responded to a desire that was part of my nature. The desire led me to a lifetime of hunting and, now, a responsibility to pass the hunting heritage forward to others born with the same aspiration. The responsibility includes understanding how the opportunity reached each of us and fully appreciating the value of the legacy.

Most of us took to the field without a thought to the notion that we were connected to Pleistocene hunters pursing mammoths across the Bering plain, peasants of old England, barons at Runnymede, our revolutionary founding fathers, oyster gatherers of the New Jersey meadowlands, a robust President with a passion to hunt, farsighted legislators, gutsy game wardens, and dedicated managers who fought for our resource. While some of those connections take a little imagination to contemplate, they are real. When we take to the fields, forests, and marshes, the deeds of these people are reflected in the freedom we have to hunt and in the game available to us. When we go afield to hunt wild game produced by the good earth, we search among the absolute truths held by the land, and the land, responding only to the law of nature, cannot be deceived.

It is always someone's turn to prepare the North American hunting heritage for its transition to the next generation. Across this vast continent there are always young people about to take aim at a sparrow. As veteran hunters, we have feasted on a wild bounty born of sacrifice and accomplishment as deep as our nation's history. It is time to shoulder the responsibility that comes with the privileges that are ours. As hunters of the North American commons, we are bound to both the deeds of our predecessors and the expectations of our heirs. We must recover the common purpose that once existed among the institutions of the hunt. Finally, we must search among ourselves for the next Roosevelt, the new Leopold, another "Ding" Darling, and please, one more Ernie Swift.

This hunting tradition and the conservation ethic within that tradition covered a lot of ground before it got to us. It passed through the hands of people both humble and great, simple and profound. This legacy did not come to our generation to die. To keep it alive, we must learn the stories, we must appreciate their significance, and we must teach each successive generation how this heritage was delivered into our custody.

If we do these things, this will be our North American hunter ethic. No one knowing these things could be disrespectful of either

- the animals placed in our custody, or
- the trust we place in one another.

It is a big order, but then the prize is enormous. The prize is already alive in wildlife all across our continent. It is the anticipation of waiting for the sun to light an October marsh; it is the heart-pounding rush that comes with a musty whiff of elk in heavy timber; it is the adrenaline surge when the gobbler calls back from deep in the spring woods. It is what moved the hair on your neck when hooves rustled dry autumn leaves; it was the mist that filled your eyes when geese, their wings locked, emerged from the November fog—and you let them pass. The people who brought these things to you were big people not afraid to dream, and their dream must have been . . . well, it must have been— mammoth.

NOTES

1 Leopold, Aldo. *A Sand County Almanac with Essays on Conservation from Round River.* New York: Oxford University Press, 1949.

2 Zakin, Susan. "Back to the Pleistocene." *Sports Afield,* February 1996.

3 Threlfall, William. "Conservation and Wildlife Policy in Britain." In *Wildlife Conservation Policy,* ed. Valerius Geist and Ian Mc-Taggart-Cowan. Calgary, Alberta: Detselig Enterprises, Ltd., 1995.

4 Nash, Roderick Frazier. *The Rights of Nature.* Madison: University of Wisconsin Press, 1981.

5 Threlfall (See reference 3).

6 Ibid.

7 Associated Press. "Protestors Closing in on Britain's Fox Hunters." *Great Falls Tribune,* December 26, 1993.

8 Grun, Bernard. *The Timetables of History.* New York: Simon and Schuster, 1982.

9 Nash (See reference 4).

10 Ibid.

11 Kosack, Joe. *The Pennsylvania Game Commission 1895-1995: 100 Years of Wildlife Conservation.* Harrisburg, PA: The Pennsylvania Game Commission, 1995.

12 Ibid.

13 Tober, James A. *Who Owns the Wildlife: The Political Economy of Conservation in Nineteenth-century America.* Westport, CT: Greenwood Press, 1981.

14 Martin v. Waddell 41 U.S. 367

15 Ibid.

16 Ibid.

17 Platt, Herman K. "With Rivers and Harbors Unsurpassed: New Jersey and Her Tidelands, 1860-1870." *New Jersey History,* Fall/Winter 1981.

18 Bean, Michael. *The Evolution of Wildlife Law.* Westport, CT: Praeger Publishers, 1949.

19 Kosack (See reference 11).

20 Haynes, Thomas. "Bison Hunting in the Yellowstone Drainage 1800-1885." (senior thesis, Montana State University, 1996).

21 Brownell, Joan Louise. "The Genesis of Wildlife Conservation in Montana." (master's thesis, Montana State University, 1987).

22 Picton, Harold and Irene. *Saga of the Sun.* Helena, MT: Montana Department of Fish and Game, 1975.

23 Neihardt, John G. *Black Elk Speaks.* Lincoln, NE: University of Nebraska Press, 1961.

24 Kosack (See reference 11)

25 Day, Donald. *The Hunting and Exploring Adventures of Theodore Roosevelt, Told in His Own Words.* New York: The Dial Press, 1955.

26 Ibid.

27 Schullery, Paul. *Theodore Roosevelt: Wilderness Writings.* Salt Lake City, UT: Peregrine Smith Books, 1986.

28 Ibid.

29 Ibid.

30 Ibid.

31 Ibid.

32 Reiger, John F. *American Sportsmen and the Origins of Conservation.* Tulsa, OK: University of Oklahoma Press, 1986.

33 Wild, Peter. *Pioneer Conservationists of Eastern America.* Missoula, MT: Mountain Press Publishing Company, 1986.

34 Williamson, Lonnie L. *Evolution of a Landmark Law.* Washington, D.C.: Department of Interior, Fish and Wildlife Service, 1987.

35 Messelt, Tom. *A Layman and Wildlife: A Layman and Wilderness.* Great Falls, MT: Self-published, 1971.

36 "State Wildlife Federation Formed, Great Falls Man President." *Helena* (Montana) *Independent,* May 17, 1936.

37 Went, Richard. *Return to the Big Grass.* Ducks Unlimited, Inc., 1987.

38 Chizek, Jim. *Game Warden Centurion.* Lodi, WI: Flambeau River Publishing, 1992.

39 Leopold (See reference 1).

40 Ibid.

41 Leopold, Aldo. *Game Management.* New York: Charles Scribner's Sons, 1948.

42 Schullery (See reference 27).

43 Trefethen, James. *An American Crusade for Wildlife.* Alexandria, VA: Boone and Crockett Club, 1975.

44 Musgrave and Stein. *Sate Wildlife Laws Handbook.* Rockville, MD: Government Industries, Inc., 1993.

ABOUT ORION–THE HUNTERS INSITITUTE

Orion–The Hunters Institute is a non-profit organization created to sustain hunting and resources essential to that purpose. National in scope, the institute works to assure ethical and responsible hunting. This effort begins with individual hunters, extends to agencies responsible for the environments in which hunting occurs, and includes those responsible for public trust in fish and wildlife. For more information, write Orion–The Hunters Institute, P.O. Box 5088, Helena, Montana 59604, or call 406-449-2795.

ABOUT THE AUTHOR

Jim Posewitz founded Orion—The Hunters Institute in 1993 after a 32-year career as a biologist with the Montana Department of Fish, Wildlife & Parks. He led the agency's ecological program for fifteen years, and he has served on boards of numerous conservation groups. His intense interest in the essence of the hunt and the history of the hunter-conservationist led to his appointment as an adjunct professor of history and philosophy at Montana State University. The university also presented him with its Blue-Gold Award for "distinguished services which have contributed to benefit mankind." He lives in Helena, Montana.

BEYOND FAIR CHASE

Jim Posewitz's first book on hunting, *Beyond Fair Chase: The Ethic and Tradition of Hunting,* is a best seller with more than 300,000 copies in print. *Beyond Fair Chase* is a "how-to" hunting book, but with a difference. It explains all aspects of hunting from gun safety to field care of game, but it binds together this information with an ethical message that is crucial for

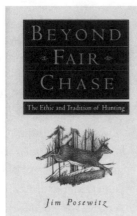

the future of hunting. Praised as "essential reading" by many hunters and non-hunters alike, *Beyond Fair Chase* is used in hunter education programs in 44 states. To order the hardcover edition, please check with your local bookstore or call The Globe Pequot Press at 1-800-962-0973, or on the Internet visit www.falcon outdoors.com. For information on the special softcover edition for hunter education programs, please call Globe Pequot.